INDIE AUTHOR MAGAZINE

HELLO AND WELCOME!

I'm Indie Annie, and I'm thrilled you're reading this gorgeous full-color version of IAM. Did you know that you can also access all the information, education, and inspiration in our app? It's available on both the iOS App Store and Google Play. And for those that prefer to listen to me read articles, you can pop over to Spotify or our website.
Happy Reading!

IndieAuthorMagazine

I0106243

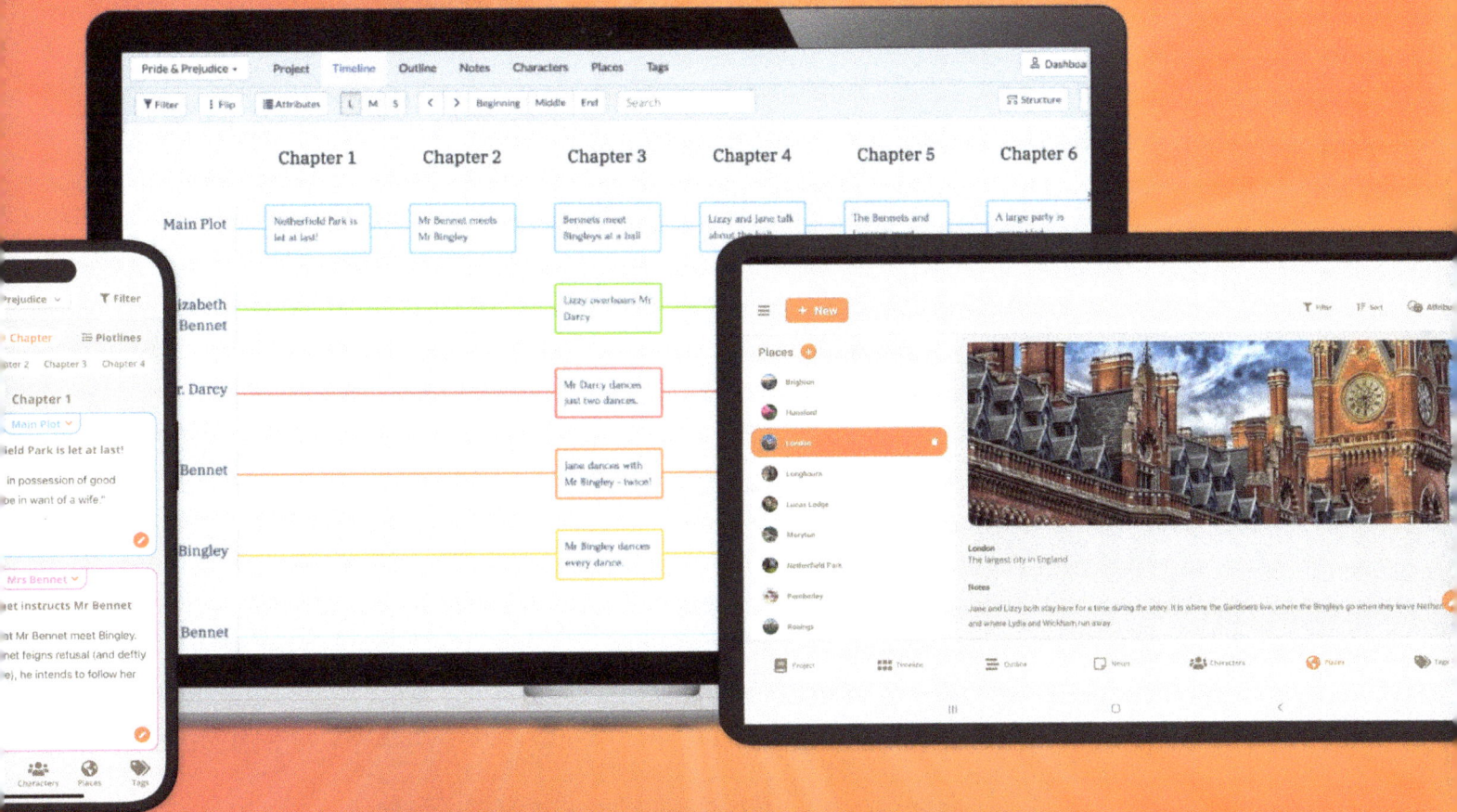

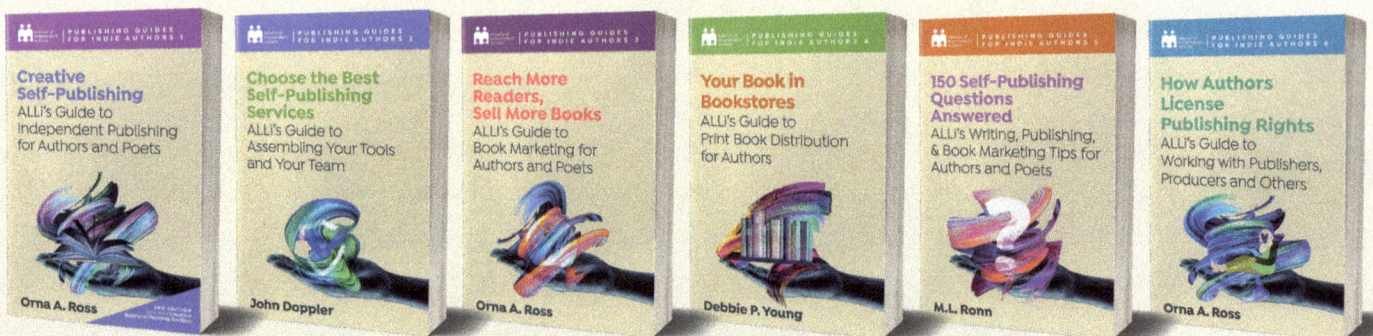

"I joined while having a crisis with Amazon KDP... The Alliance is a beacon of light. I recommend that all indie authors join...
Susan Marshall

"The Alliance is about standing together.
Joanna Penn

"It's the good stuff, all on one place.
Richard Wright

"ALLi has helped me in myriad ways: discounts on services, vetting providers, charting a course to sales success. But more than anything it's a community of friendly, knowledgeable, helpful people."
Beth Duke

See hundreds more testimonials at:
AllianceIndependentAuthors.org/testimonials

IAM
FORMATS

12   Editor's Letter: Formats of the Future

14   Martelle's Motivation: Bending the Universe to Your Will

16   ALLi Exclusive

18   Dear Indie Annie: Frugal Formatter

20   Ten Tips: Hiring a Book Formatter

24   Celeste Barclay Makes Your Granny Blush

30   Narrators Share the Audiobook Prep You Should Do Before You Hit 'Record'

34   Edging Out the Competition: Exploring Design Options for Special or Limited Edition Print Books

40   Craft Consistency with a Style Bible for Book Formatting

44   An Answer to AI Audiobook Debates? Sounded Walks the Ethical Tightrope

48   From the Stacks

49   Crafting Dialogue Tags that Disappear: Best Practices for Your Prose

52   Prosperity: More Formats, More Options, More Money

54   Two Birds, One Net Gain: How Nature Can Improve Your Health and Your Writing

56   Corner the Market: Free Money—or Close to It

The Self Publishing Show LIVE!

THE SOUTHBANK CENTRE, LONDON
25TH & 26TH JUNE 2024

Once again sponsored by Amazon KDP and attended by hundreds of authors plus major industry players, Europe's premier indie author conference is going to be bigger and better than ever. The 2024's two day schedule is now confirmed with EL James, Lucy Score, Steve Higgs, Sasha Black, Craig Martelle, Rachel McLean and many more.

TICKETS AVAILABLE NOW: learnselfpublishing.com/spslive

SPS Live 2024
SCHEDULE

kindle direct publishing
SELF-PUBLISH IN DIGITAL & PRINT

THE SELF PUBLISHING SHOW LIVE! LONDON 2024

DAY 1 – TUESDAY 25TH JUNE 2024

9.00 AM	WELCOME - JAMES BLATCH
9.10 AM	YOU CAN TOO! - STEVE HIGGS
9.45 AM	THE FIVE SECRETS OF FINDING YOUR AUDIENCE - SUZY K QUINN
10.30 AM	BREAK
11.00 AM	3 STRATEGIES TO PROMOTE NEW RELEASES WITH BOOKBUB ADS - AUDREY DEROBERT
11.35 AM	AI: FEAR, LOATHING & ACCEPTANCE - JAMES BLATCH
12.10 PM	LSP COURSES UPDATE - RICARDO FAYET & JAMES BLATCH
12.30 PM	LUNCH
1.30 PM	CRACKING THE AUDIOBOOK CODE - CRAIG THOMSON
2.15 PM	HOOKING ONE MILLION READERS - E.L. JAMES & LUCY SCORE
3.00 PM	BREAK
3.30 PM	THE FUTURE OF AUDIO BOOKS PANEL - RACHEL MCLEAN, MILES STEVENS-HOARE FROM WF HOWES, VICTORIA GERKEN FROM PODIUM AUDIO & WILL DAGES FROM FINDAWAY VOICES FROM SPOTIFY
4.35 PM	GENERATIVE AI & EDITING - CHRIS BANKS
5.15 PM	FINISH

DAY 2 – WEDNESDAY 26TH JUNE 2024

9.00 AM	DAY 2 INTRODUCTION - JAMES BLATCH
9.05 AM	BECOMING FULL-TIME WITH KDP - HANNH LYNN, CLARE LYDON AND SASHA BLACK
9.50 AM	FINDING HUNGRY READERS - ALEX NEWTON
10.25 AM	EFFECTIVELY USING EMAIL PROMOS: FROM INBOX TO BESTSELLER - MIKE HOURIGAN
11.00 AM	BREAK
11.30 AM	DEEP DIVE INTO AUDIBLE - LEE JARIT
12.05 PM	UNLOCKING THE POTENTIAL OF YOUR AUTHOR WEBSITE - STUART GRANT
12.50 PM	THE NEXT STEP IN YOUR AUTHOR CAREER - RACHEL MCLEAN
1.30 PM	LUNCH
2.30 PM	WIDEN YOUR WORLD - DAN WOOD
3.05 PM	THE DIRECT SELLING ECOSYSTEM - DAMON COURTNEY
3.50 PM	DEALING WITH CHANGE - CRAIG MARTELLE
4.20 PM	GOODBYE - JAMES BLATCH
4.40 PM	FINISH

Please note:
Conference sessions are subject to change at short notice.

LONDON

Authorpreneurs in Action

"I love Lulu! They've been a fantastic distributor of my paperbacks and an excellent partner as I dive into direct sales. They integrate so smoothly with my personal Shopify store, and their customer support has been top notch."

Katie Cross, katiecrossbooks.com

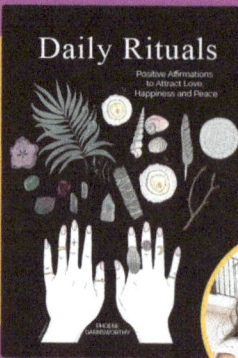

"Having my own store has given me the freedom to look at my creativity as a profitable business and lifelong career."

Phoebe Garnsworthy, phoebegarnsworthy.com

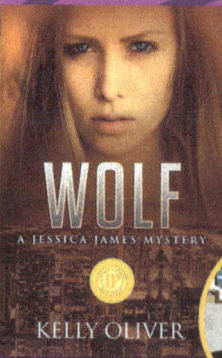

"Lulu has a super handy integration with Shopify. Lulu makes it so easy to sell paperbacks directly to readers."

Kelly Oliver, kellyoliverbooks.com

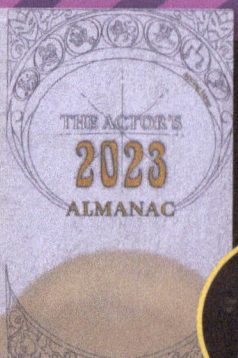

"My experience with Lulu Direct has been more convenient and simple than I anticipated or thought possible. I simply publish, take a step back and allow the well-oiled machine to run itself. Most grateful!"

Molly McGivern, theactorsalmanac.com

INDIE
AUTHOR MAGAZINE

EDITORIAL

Publisher | Chelle Honiker

Editor in Chief | Nicole Schroeder

Creative Director | Alice Briggs

ADVERTISING & MARKETING

Inquiries
Ads@AtheniaCreative.com

Information
https://IndieAuthorMagazine.com/
advertising/

CONTRIBUTORS

Angela Archer, Elaine Bateman, Patricia Carr, Bradley Charbonneau, Honorée Corder, Jackie Dana, Heather Clement Davis, Jamie Davis, Laurel Decher, Fatima Fayez, Gill Fernley, Greg Fishbone, Jen B. Green, Jac Harmon, Marion Hermannsen, Steve Higgs, Chrishaun Keller-Hanna, Kasia Lasinska, Monica Leonelle, Jenn Lessmann, Megan Linski-Fox, Craig Martelle, Angie Martin, Merri Maywether, Kevin McLaughlin, Lasairiona McMaster, Jenn Mitchell, Tanya Nellestein, Russell Nohelty, Susan Odev, Eryka Parker, Tiffany Robinson, Clare Sager, Joe Solari, Becca Syme, David Viergutz

SUBSCRIPTIONS
https://indieauthormagazine.com/subscribe/

HOW TO READ
https://indieauthormagazine.com/how-to-read/

WHEN WRITING MEANS BUSINESS
IndieAuthorMagazine.com

Athenia Creative | 6820 Apus Dr., Sparks, NV, 89436 USA | 775.298.1925

ISSN 2768-7880 (online)–ISSN 2768-7872 (print)

Remember when the publishing industry was at odds about whether e-books would replace print books? It's an almost comical debate to consider now, given how integral both are to many of our careers. But it's far from the only time the book world has pitted one format against another. Just look at the posts on Instagram and TikTok today about whether listening to audiobooks counts as reading, or consider the way readers will snap up specialty hardcover editions of a series they already own in paperback.

Before any of us became authors ourselves, we probably never stopped to consider what goes into creating these extra editions. After all, it's all the same story, right? But as you likely know, and as this month's articles highlight, each new format we release costs time, effort, and often money. E-books need to adhere to different requirements on each platform. Special editions take additional internal formatting or cover elements to stand out. Audiobooks may require you to prep information sheets before handing the manuscript off to a narrator or make edits to the story itself if you opt for a full-cast narration.

None of this is to say extra formats are required; as always, the decision of what's best for your business rests in your hands. But as software tools, specialty formatters, and AI audio platforms make other formats more accessible to authors, it will be interesting to see whether the editions we view as "standard" will expand once more, like they have since the e-book vs. paperback debate first raged.

Even in this potential future, there's a cost to every new version of a story that's released. That will never change. But neither will the fact that each new format can connect us with new audiences of readers, or with our current audience in new ways. Whether it's part of your usual production in the future or an optional business decision you make today, all that work can be worth it—no debate or comparison needed.

Nicole Schroeder
Editor in Chief
Indie Author Magazine

Nicole Schroeder is a storyteller at heart. As the editor in chief of Indie Author Magazine, she brings nearly a decade of journalism and editorial experience to the publication, delighting in any opportunity to tell true stories and help others do the same. She holds a bachelor's degree from the Missouri School of Journalism and minors in English and Spanish. Her previous work includes editorial roles at local publications, and she's helped edit and produce numerous fiction and nonfiction books, including a Holocaust survivor's memoir, alongside independent publishers. Her own creative writing has been published in national literary magazines. When she's not at her writing desk, Nicole is usually in the saddle, cuddling her guinea pigs, or spending time with family. She loves any excuse to talk about Marvel movies and considers National Novel Writing Month its own holiday.

MARTELLE'S MOTIVATION

Bending the Universe to Your Will

Dominate! Master the process. Work hard.
One hundred percent of your effort must go to winning, but the only battle you'll win is the same one fought within each of us. You win against yourself—not others.

As an author, it's inevitable that your readers will compare you to their favorites and that you will compare yourself to your peers. Readers comparing you is simply marketing. Your reputation is how your readers see you because they are the ones paying your salary.

It's a long and slippery slope if you battle other authors, no matter what they say about you or do in their careers.

Each one of us can bend the universe to our will, but in the universe of ourselves, we are the one and only resident. How we respond to challenges and how we work today to set ourselves up for a better tomorrow is completely up to us, no matter the situation we face.

Don't risk what you can't afford to lose. Every day is a calculation of energy to expend toward a goal, and whether it gets you one step closer or twenty, all that matters is that you keep moving forward. That's you taking charge of your destiny. When you refuse to let the noise hold you back, that's the force of your will.

There's only so much fight in us. Don't waste it on things that don't get you to your goal. Your energy is limited. Your force of will gets stronger with use but weakens with misuse. Apply it liberally to those efforts that keep you moving forward. You'll find your energy quickly wanes when you try to fight all the battles, which leaves you nothing for the greater good of your own existence.

Fight the good fight, but fight it for yourself.

Let your force of will move the mountains that are in your way. You don't have to move the whole range, only the obstacles before you. Surmount them one by one, and keep going.

We lose when we stop, even if we feel like we're not making any progress.

Have you fought battles that didn't help you? How much energy do you have left?

Don't waste it. ■

Craig Martelle

Craig Martelle

High school Valedictorian enlists in the Marine Corps under a guaranteed tank contract. An inauspicious start that was quickly superseded by excelling in language study. Contract waived, a year at the Defense Language Institute to learn Russian and off to keep my ears on the big red machine during the Soviet years. Earned a four-year degree in two years by majoring in Russian Language. My general staff. career included choice side gigs - UAE, Bahrain, Korea, Russia, and Ukraine.

Major Martelle. I retired from the Marines after a couple years at the embassy in Moscow working arms control issues.

Department of Homeland Security then law school next. I was working for a high-end consulting firm performing business diagnostics, business law, and leadership coaching. For the money they paid me, I was good with that. Just until I wasn't. Then I started writing.

ALLI EXCLUSIVE

One Story Takes Many Forms

What book formats should an author be creating? Doesn't it just come down to print, e-books, and audio? Well, no; there are a lot of exciting variations to explore under the broad heading of "formats." The Alliance of Independent Authors (ALLi) does of course offer detailed advice on each of those three categories, but in addition to that, it also can provide information on a number of alternative editions authors can incorporate into their production process. It's about choosing which formats to pay attention to as you begin and as you grow your author business.

BEGINNER AUTHORS: GET THE BASICS IN PLACE

Occasionally beginner authors will focus more on paperbacks because they want to feel like they have a "real" book in their hands, or they'll put more effort toward e-books because they can be quicker and cheaper to format and arrange cover designs for. But ALLi recommends authors immediately offer both formats so as to maximize their sales: print—usually paperback, though hardbacks are also available—and e-books. Below are links that will guide you through both formats, but make sure to also arrange for minor formatting variations, which allow you to access wider platforms. Paperbacks for Amazon, for instance, will require a slightly different cover layout than other platforms, such as IngramSpark, to adhere to each distributor's template. This will allow you to broaden your reach to wholesale catalogs, which means the ability to distribute to libraries and bookshops, as well as new retail platforms.

For e-book creation, ALLi takes you through each step of the process here: https://selfpublishingadvice.org/how-to-publish-an-ebook.

For print books, ALLi's detailed formatting guide can be found at: https://selfpublishingadvice.org/the-ultimate-guide-to-formatting-your-print-book.

EMERGING AUTHORS: DEVELOP AUDIO AND TRANSLATED WORKS

If you've built the foundation of your author career, now is the time to consider whether you have the budget for two additional formats that can carry greater expense and/or time input: audiobooks and translations.

Audiobooks have been a growing market for some time, and many readers appreciate having this format available to them, either out of personal preference or accessibility needs. Whether you narrate your books yourself or choose a narrator to work with, this format requires additional time and money, but it can bring your book alive in a new way. Working with a narrator gives you the opportunity to request a short promotional message, which can work well when advertising the title, such as in book trailers or on your website. Read ALLi's blog post, "The Ultimate Guide to Audiobooks for Authors," at https://selfpublishingadvice.org for everything you need.

For children's authors, the new Yoto audio cards for younger listeners are growing in popularity and can be a great format to tap into. Parents can buy blank cards and "make their own" by downloading and linking MP3 files, so once you have your audiobook, it's worth mentioning this possibility on your website and when marketing to parents.

Translations are also a growing area of interest within the indie community. Germany has been an early success story, but consider which languages have the greatest global application, such as Spanish. Again, there is a choice of arranging the translation yourself, with a professional translator, or of licensing the translation rights if you have already proven the book does well in English markets.

For ALLi's complete guide to translations, visit: https://selfpublishingadvice.org/the-ultimate-guide-to-book-translations-for-indie-authors.

EXPERIENCED AUTHORS: MAKE SOMETHING BEAUTIFUL … AND LICENSE IT

Experienced authors may wish to explore additional ways of connecting with their growing readership base and developing new income streams—for example, via Patreon or Kickstarter. These platforms and approaches offer the opportunity to create hardbacks or other premium formats of books for loyal readers and backers, as well as items such as companion workbooks for nonfiction. ALLi has a guide to creating such premium offerings, from clothbound to leather, with options to add embellishments, such as foil. These premium details allow authors to offer something truly special, elevating their books beyond standard formats and appealing to younger generations, who show a preference for specialty printed books thanks to the influence of social media platforms like TikTok, where displaying physical books is an important part of the aesthetic.

Learn more about creating hardback or special edition formats at: https://selfpublishingadvice.org/the-ultimate-guide-to-hardback-and-premium-books.

Finally, remember that each format you create can be licensed into different languages, and you can exploit your intellectual property to expand into entirely new mediums, including films, TV, games, apps, merchandise, and more. Explore ALLi's book *How Authors Sell Publishing Rights* to look into the opportunities available to you. Visit https://selfpublishingadvice.org/bookshop/rights-licensing.

Formats might initially seem like something only beginners need to consider, but in truth, taking the time to explore all format options available to you at any stage is always a good move for a successful author.

Melissa Addey, ALLi Campaigns Manager

Melissa Addey, ALLi Campaigns Manager

The Alliance of Independent Authors (ALLi) is a global membership association for self-publishing authors. A non-profit, our mission is ethics and excellence in self-publishing. Everyone on our team is a working indie author and we offer advice and advocacy for self-publishing authors within the literary, publishing and creative industries around the world. www.allianceindependentauthors.org

DEAR INDIE ANNIE,

In the past, I've hired editors, cover designers, and even a virtual assistant. Passing off those responsibilities makes sense, but internal formatting always seems so straightforward. At what point is it worth investing in professional formatting services?

Frugal Formatter

Dear Frugal,

Oh my, that moniker sounds like you're an inhabitant of Middle Earth, but I digress. Formatting your own manuscript seems as simple as building a bookcase from IKEA: just insert tab A into slot B, right? A practical task any common or garden hobbit could master. But that DIY approach can leave your literary furnishings looking a bit, shall we say, homely? Let's review when it pays to hire a professional carpenter versus handling the handiwork yourself.

For simple structures like novellas or nonfiction, your homemade formatting may suffice. Bold chapter heads, page numbers, basic styling—these are achievable weekend projects for industrious authors willing to learn. But for complex novels brimming with plot twists and intricate world-building, you may want to consider hiring a master carpenter. Professionals with eagle eyes for detail can elevate your presentation from mundane to majestic.

Formatting fiction requires particular finesse, and dialogue formatting, scene breaks, and clever use of white space take skills that DIYers may lack. Your end table may have worked fine with one or two screws left over, but skipping any formatting steps when constructing your finished book could result in a disjointed reading experience. Don't allow lackluster layouts to overshadow brilliant prose. It's okay to let those in the trade handle the meticulous finishing.

Most importantly, labor should lift your spirits, not drain them. As Irish playwright and critic George Bernard Shaw said, "Nothing is worth doing unless the consequences may be serious." Shoddy formatting has real consequences for readership enjoyment, and tedious tasks can also kill your writer spirit. If you enjoy these tasks and want to develop your skill set, that's great. But there's no shame in seeking help.

For standard digital and print distribution, DIY formatting may suffice if you invest time honing those skills or have a program that can handle the basics. But for special editions sold directly through your website or other exclusive projects, a professional's expertise

can vastly elevate your presentation. Imagine offering signed copies of a new release with a stylish print layout. What about bundling an e-book with a print companion book designed with gorgeous aesthetics? Limited-run hard copies with bonus materials like author notes and illustrations require creative layout mastery. Let a pro handle minute details like embellished drop caps, ornate frames, and other touches readers crave on prized editions.

Particularly for debut authors, presentation matters immensely when introducing your work to readers. You may choose to distinguish yourself from the masses with imaginative formatting that captivates fans, or you may want someone with more expertise to walk you through the process and everything you need to consider the first time through it. Of course, Frugal, it sounds like you've published before, but even for passion projects close to your heart, you may want to bring in a master carpenter so the construction matches the quality of the content. Then you can focus your creative energies on the writing craft itself. Together, you can construct literary architecture built to last!

If you do decide to hire a professional formatter for your next work, there are a few best practices to note. When hiring formatters, ask to see samples of previous work. Request a style guide outlining their process.

Explain exactly what you want: print layouts, e-book files, etc. Ask how many rounds of changes are included. Be very clear on needs before starting.

Provide excerpts for them to demonstrate their ability. If the sample dazzles you, they likely have the skills you need to elevate your whole book.

Formatting partnerships require trust and communication. Voice concerns promptly if work underwhelms. A true professional welcomes constructive feedback for improvement.

In summary, you ask if hiring an experienced formatter is worth the money, and my answer, dear one, is that it is if it will save you valuable writing time, and/or will help your books stand out in a crowded market, and/ or you want to treat your fans to limited and special editions. Do the math. It may also be worth it purely for its aesthetic appeal and how it makes your hobbit heart flutter. Imagine the joy of holding a beautifully formatted special edition in your hands. Sound good? Then it's worth it.

Happy writing,
Indie Annie X

10 TIPS FOR
HIRING A BOOK FORMATTER

Your book is finally finished, and it's been edited to within an inch of its life. But you're not quite ready to publish yet. As well as a quality, genre-specific cover, you're going to need to get your book formatted for every way you want to publish it: e-book, paperback print, large print, hardback, or more.

With programs like Atticus and Vellum making formatting more accessible, plenty of authors choose to tackle formatting themselves. But if you're looking for something that goes beyond the basic layout options provided by these platforms, or if you simply don't want to wrestle with formatting on your own, it may be worth it to hire a book formatter to do the work for you. If you've never hired a formatter before, never fear! Read on for ten tips for getting started.

1 DECIDE WHETHER YOU NEED A PROFESSIONAL FORMATTER

Consider whether the expense of a professional formatter feels worth the investment. This is, as always, your book business, and you are an individual with different skills, talents, and aptitudes. Maybe you're an expert in formatting, and you have plenty of time for it in your schedule. Great! You probably don't need to hire someone.

However, if bleeds, widows and orphans, trim size, and kerning are a complete mystery to you, you may need some help. But it's not only about knowing how to do basic formatting. For some books, particularly some nonfiction, you may need a more complex layout with images, maps, and diagrams that will need a professional touch. And unless formatting is one of your specialties, if you're creating a special edition book with colored pages, chapter graphics, gold leaf, and all the trimmings, it can be worth paying a professional to get the high-end finish you're looking for.

2 FIND A BOOK FORMATTER TO HIRE

One of the best ways to find a trusted formatter is to ask other authors for recommendations. That way, you can be sure you're working with a business that has proven results and satisfied customers. Even if your fellow authors go the DIY route, however, you can still find formatting services on sites like Fiverr, Upwork, and Reedsy. Before you hire someone, check their feedback and star ratings, if the site offers them. Also consider the following:

- Do they have experience in your genre?
- Does their portfolio appeal to you and suit your author branding?
- Are they experienced?
- Can they explain things to you clearly and in plain English, if you need that?
- Do you think you will get along? That may not matter for a one-off job, but it will if you're planning on working with this person for the long term.

3 LOOK FOR RED FLAGS

When hiring anyone new for your business, do your due diligence to vet them beforehand. We could make a list of red flags to watch for—and we have:

- poor communication;
- poor reviews mentioning examples of poor customer service or rude behavior—most people will get the odd one- or two-star review, simply because you can't please everybody, but too many can be a big red flag;
- no portfolio or a very poor one;
- no clear list of what the service includes; or
- drama—it might be entertaining at first, but it will wear on you quickly if you're looking for a long-term business partner.

4 CONSIDER YOUR BUDGET

As with any hired service, prices can vary widely for professional formatting. Some professional book formatters on Fiverr list their services for as low as $10, but pro services—"offered by free-lancers vetted for their skills and expertise by a dedicated Fiverr Pro team," according to the site—start around $140, at the time of writing.

Do your research and bear your budget in mind, and you should be able to find someone suitable that you can afford, though expect to spend around a couple hundred dollars on standard formatting services, according to Kindlepreneur.

Pro Tip: You may save money if your formatter offers bundles, where you can, for example, get your e-book and print book done together for a lower price.

5   CHECK WHAT YOUR SERVICE INCLUDES

When hiring someone, look at the list of services they'll provide in your package to see if there's any work you'll need to take on afterward.

Check how many revisions you get and whether you'll receive the source files, so you can make changes later without having to pay again or pass the files onto a new formatter if a problem develops with the original.

You must also hire a formatter that uses fonts licensed for commercial use. A book is a commercial product, and you can't use personal-use-only fonts to produce your books.

Pro Tip: Pay attention to the turnaround time your formatter offers. You can't afford to be waiting for your final formatted files when your preorder upload deadline is rushing toward you.

6   MAKE SURE YOU HAVE A CONTRACT

If you're paying a formatter directly, then as a professional business, they should have a standard contract that they use. If they don't, you could find a quality downloadable contract or have your lawyer write a standard one that you can use for service providers. Lay out every expectation on both sides, including how long it will take, what is included, how much it will cost, refunds and guarantees, what happens if either of you needs to pull out of the project, and other relevant agreements. If you're using a site such as Fiverr, this will be taken care of for you to an extent, but scan what's included, and ask as many questions as you'd like before handing over any cash.

7   CONSIDER YOUR GENRE

Hopefully, you know your own genre well enough to know what a typical interior looks like, including whether chapter heading graphics are used, what the usual fonts and font sizes are, and other formatting standards. It's ideal if you can find a formatter with experience in your genre. They may come up with designs and formatting that you have not considered but that are still very much genre suitable. They should also know what's trending; especially if you're new to book publishing, that knowledge can be invaluable.

8   PLAN TO FORMAT FOR EACH EDITION

Each edition of your book will require different formatting that your formatter should understand. You may lose some of the fancier design with an e-book version, or have to change fonts from the print version to allow e-book readers to adjust the font and size of the text.

Your formatter should be an expert on this and should be able to advise you if you ask for something that won't work. They should also be able to produce a set of books that look like they belong together, despite the differences in each format.

9 HELP YOUR FORMATTER WHERE YOU CAN

Ideally, it's good to collect a quality team of people you can rely on for book formatting, cover design, and other publishing and marketing jobs. However, if you drive your chosen formatter around the bend with poorly presented documents every single time, they may not be your formatter for very long.

Firstly, ask what your formatter needs. Find out what file formats they accept and ask them if they have any preferences in formatting on your end that will help with the task.

Send your finished book all in one document, and try to be consistent throughout your manuscript. Use a clear, common font, such as Times New Roman, and standardize the margins. Add chapter headings using Styles and Formatting rather than by manually changing the font size, style, or alignment. That simply doesn't work as well and will have to be replaced by your formatter.

Be clear on what you want. If you want the first two pages of each chapter to be black paper with white text, with a particular chapter graphic, you need to tell them that before they've started the job. If you want to publish with a range of different sites who all have different print guidelines, your formatter needs to know that up front.

10 EXPLORE OTHER OPTIONS IF NEEDED

If a professional formatter is outside of your budget, you may be able to swap services with another author or service provider. This can work out well for both of you, as long as you remember the previous points about having a contract and specifying what's included.

There are also plenty of tools and software that will allow you to handle the basics yourself. Vellum, Adobe InDesign, and Atticus have varying learning curves and prices, but they may be more accessible if you're willing to learn. Draft2Digital, among others, will also let you simply upload a DOCX file and will then format it for you and produce an EPUB for you to download. ■

Gill Fernley

Gill Fernley

Gill Fernley writes fiction in several genres under different pen names, but what all of them have in common is humor and romance, because she can't resist a happy ending or a good laugh. She's also a freelance content writer and has been running her own business since 2013. Before that, she was a technical author and documentation manager for an engineering company and can describe to you more than you'd ever wish to know about airflow and filtration in downflow booths. Still awake? Wow, that's a first! Anyway, that experience taught her how to explain complex things in straightforward language and she hopes it will come in handy for writing articles for IAM. Outside of writing, she's a cake decorator, expert shoe hoarder, and is fluent in English, dry humor and procrastibaking.

The Romances of Celeste Barclay

FROM ASPIRING TO BE A CORPORATE LAWYER TO MAKING YOUR GRANNY BLUSH

Before becoming the author of more than fifty books, Celeste Barclay earned degrees in international affairs, secondary social science, and political management. It's no surprise then that her books are so thoroughly researched and accurate. From particular Scottish clans to the hierarchy of mafia syndicates, Celeste seeks to incorporate actual history in all the books she writes.

Her research and care for her stories extends beyond her books; alongside her author career, Celeste has also served as president of Novelists, Inc. (NINC), supporting authors and other professionals from both independent and traditional publishing circles. Her work has made an impact on both sides of the book industry—making her impromptu decision to divert from her previous career and try her hand at writing years ago all the more meaningful.

THE START OF A STEAMY CAREER

Marriage and a family sidelined Celeste's initial plan to become a corporate lawyer, leading her to eventually find herself teaching English and social studies to high school students. A move to substitute teaching gave her the flexibility to take a more active role in her children's education.

"The Writing Gals [group] on Facebook was immensely helpful to me," she says. "And I joined a couple of authors' behind-the-scenes groups and forward-facing reader groups."

Celeste would launch her books at 99 cents. After a week, she would bump the books up to full price, yet she would retain the Amazon Number One New Release banner for thirty days at a time.

She kept writing for about a year and a half before realizing that not only was she wearing herself down managing both jobs, but she was also making more money writing than she was teaching. She left her day job behind and was soon discovered by Oliver-Heber Books, a small publishing house owned by author Tanya Anne Crosby.

UNVEILING THE BLUSH: BARCLAY'S UNIQUE WRITING PROCESS

Celeste writes Highlander, Viking and Pirate Historical Romances, as well as Mafia Contemporary Romances under the pen name Sabine Barclay,

Generally a planner and a strategist, Celeste surprised herself by writing her first book on a whim. "I told no one," she says. "I mean, seriously, no one. I didn't even tell my cat." An avid reader of romantic fiction, she had the impulse to try her hand at writing her own Highlander Romance. She loves rugged, alpha heroes facing life-and-death circumstances while navigating clan politics and governing their people, she says.

Celeste spent a week working on book 1 in July 2017, finished the book in February 2018, and published it in April 2018. Upon the completion of book 1, Celeste knew she had the beginning of a terrific series. Between releasing book 2 and writing book 3 of her Highlander series, Celeste began making connections with other authors, as well as getting educated on taking her writing to an entirely new level. That's when she wrote a novella lead magnet and launched her newsletter. She released book 3, and "things took off," she says.

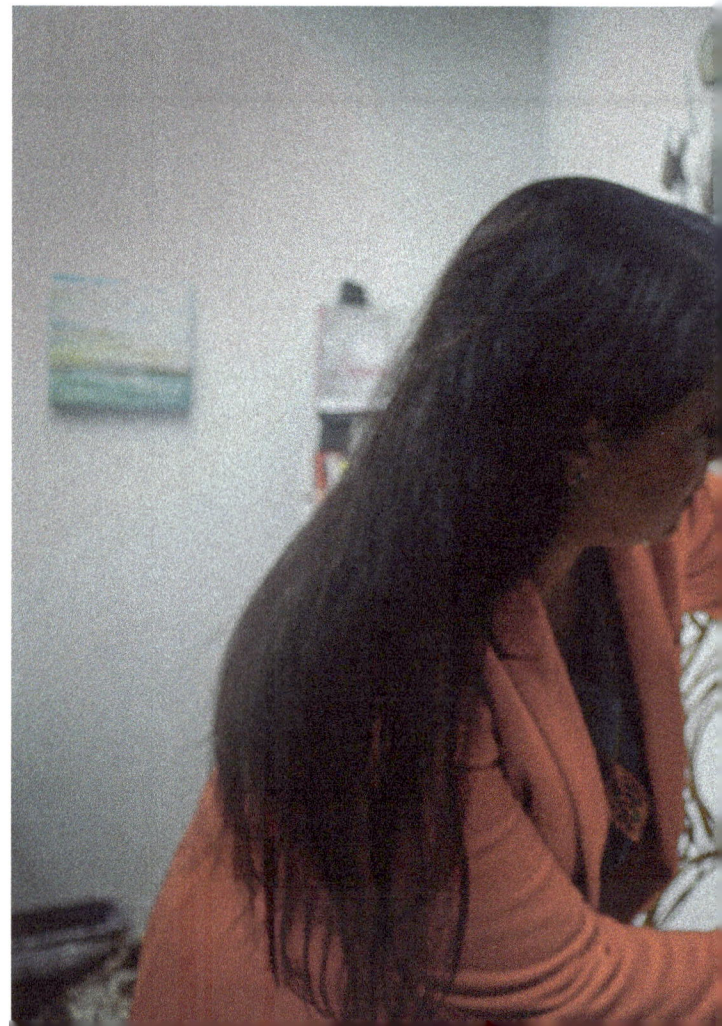

all under the Oliver-Heber Books banner. As she pens ten to fourteen books per year, I had to ask if her publisher has a hard time keeping up with her production schedule. Says Celeste, "No, they [Oliver-Heber Books] have just been so fantastic to me. I have so much freedom to write what I want, when I want, how I want."

Writing novels that are between eighty-five thousand and one hundred twenty thousand words, Celeste aims to release a book every six weeks. When asked how she plans out her book release schedule, Celeste gleefully holds up her five-year planner. Having been an educator, she plans backward from her release date. The date she delivers the book to ARC readers is two weeks back from the release date; the proofreader is two weeks back from that. She has learned to give herself more grace and to write everything in her planner in pencil.

For the sake of alleviating undue stress, she now tries to give herself bigger buffers and reassess when she needs to do so. "I'm not a particularly goal-oriented person, to be honest, because I'm very duty driven," Celeste says. She says she's intrinsically motivated, so she enjoys having a plan in place to let her know what she needs to work on next—and what she has to look forward to. At the time of this writing, that was the release of her first book in a new series, House of Clan Sutherland—book 55 of her career—and the release of *Mob Boss* under her Sabine Barclay pen name, which released March 26.

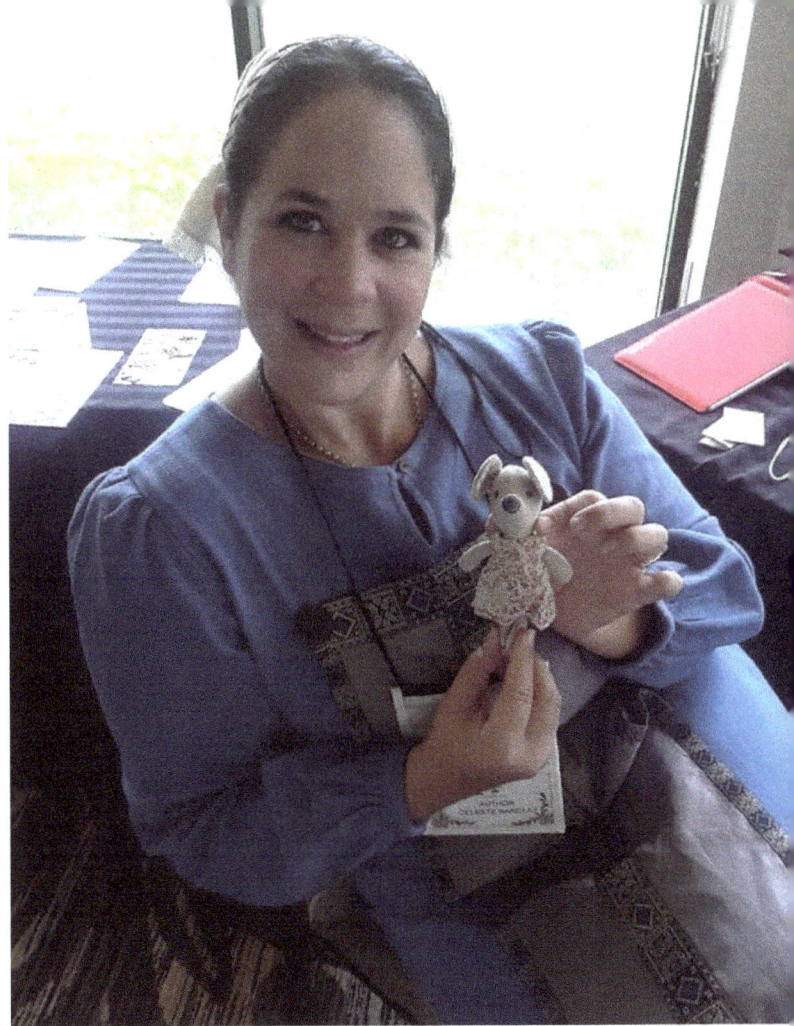

How is this "plantser"—a term Celeste uses that refers to someone who both plans and improvises their writing—so prolific? She absolutely loves writing and has a very long attention span. "I can do five thousand words or I can do twenty thousand words in a day," she says. "It just depends on how it's flowing and what I need to do. I've come to realize that is a little atypical." Even so, Celeste says she finds writing to be extremely cathartic. "I love living in my imagination. It's a fantastic place to be."

THE LEGACY OF BLUSHING GRANNIES: BARCLAY'S IMPACT ON FELLOW AUTHORS

Celeste's impact on the publishing world isn't only for the stories she publishes; just as other authors encouraged her early on, she now helps other authors find their place in the industry. Early in her writing career, Celeste became involved in NINC, a networking organization for both self-published and traditionally published novelists, as well as other publishing professionals. She started out on the nominating committee, became president-elect in 2022, and became president of the organization in 2023. She took a role in NINC as chair of the Diversity, Equity, and Inclusion Committee when she became president-elect.

When asked what separates NINC from other author organizations, Celeste explains that NINC is a curated membership. "You have to earn your way in, and the bar does not fluctuate." NINC members are professional novelists—both traditionally and indie published—who have attained the same level of experience. This ensures that, within the group, members are able to have conversations that aren't germane to less-experienced authors.

"It's not fair on the part of either party when you have folks who are newer and less experienced listening to conversations they don't understand because they're not there yet," Celeste says. "Nor is it fair to those who are trying to have a conversation at an upper level to then inadvertently exclude people or then have to bring the conversation down to make sure everybody understands."

Each year, NINC hosts a multi-day networking event for its members in St. Pete Beach, Florida. Celeste describes it as a large conference that doesn't feel like a large conference. "People are very hospitable. You meet people of all different walks of life, all different genres." This year's NINC Conference takes place September 18–22, and registration is open for NINC members until July 1.

BE FLEXIBLE, GRANNY!

When asked what advice she'd like to share with other authors, Celeste gets reflective. "Don't close the door on any opportunities. Weigh them seriously," she says. "You know, I am with a small house, but because of that I lean far more towards the indie side than New York trad. I do think that there are some genres that do still lend themselves best to trad. But I also believe that at this point, there are great opportunities across most genres."

Celeste advises authors to think about the story they want to write and then think about who they're writing for. "Don't put yourself in a position where you can't market your book because you think that it's so 'out there.' There are bound to be books that are comparable or a couple of books that, interwoven, are comparable to yours," she says. "Understand that your creativity is only part of the business. If you want to sell a book and even make a penny off of it, then those two mindsets [creativity and business] have to blend together."

Being an author was not a career Celeste aspired to—she stumbled upon it, and she's so happy she

did, she says. Being open to opportunities she was presented with and working hard to capitalize on every challenge has resulted in her having a flourishing, lucrative career that she loves. ■

Gayle Leeson

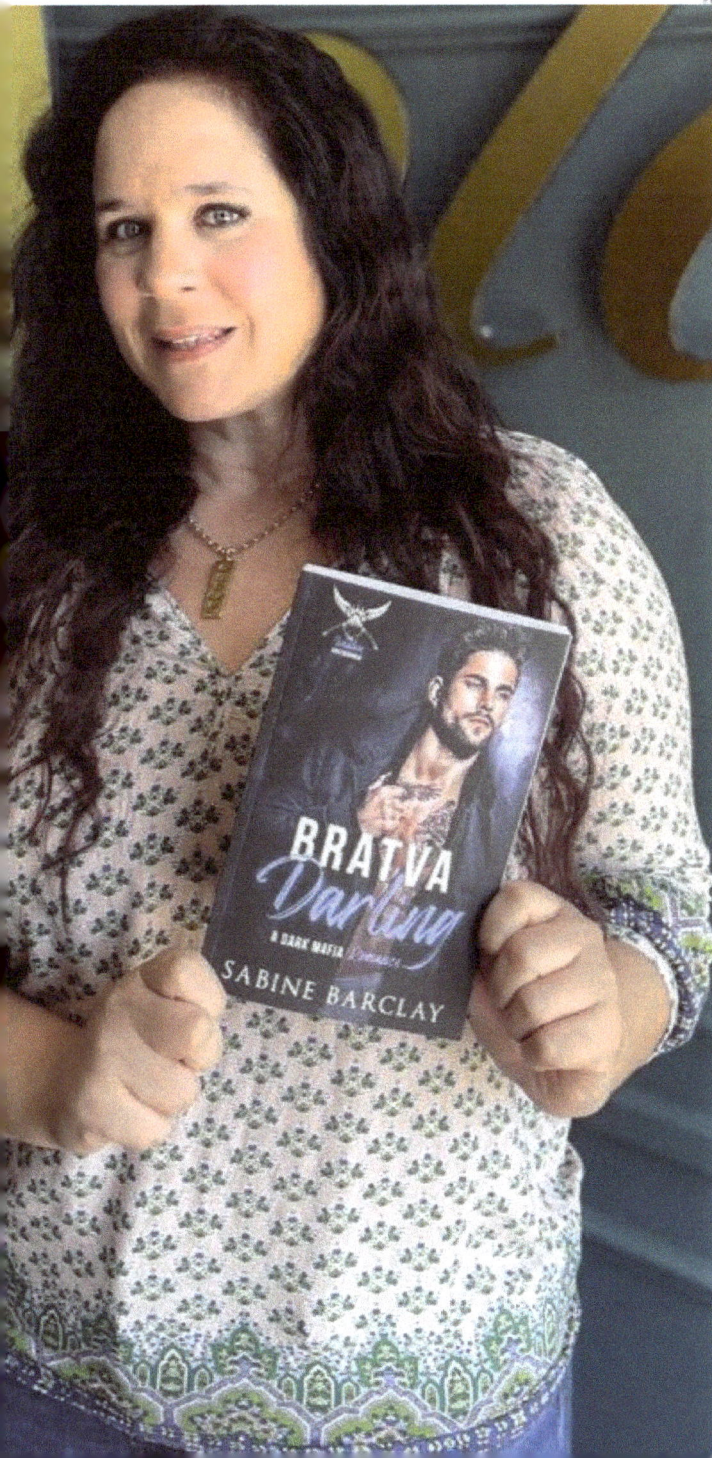

Gayle Leeson

Gayle Leeson is a USA TODAY best-selling, award-winning author who writes multiple cozy mystery series and a portal fantasy series under the pen name G. Leeson. Gayle has also written as Amanda Lee (the embroidery mystery series) and as Gayle Trent. Visit her online at gayleleeson.com.

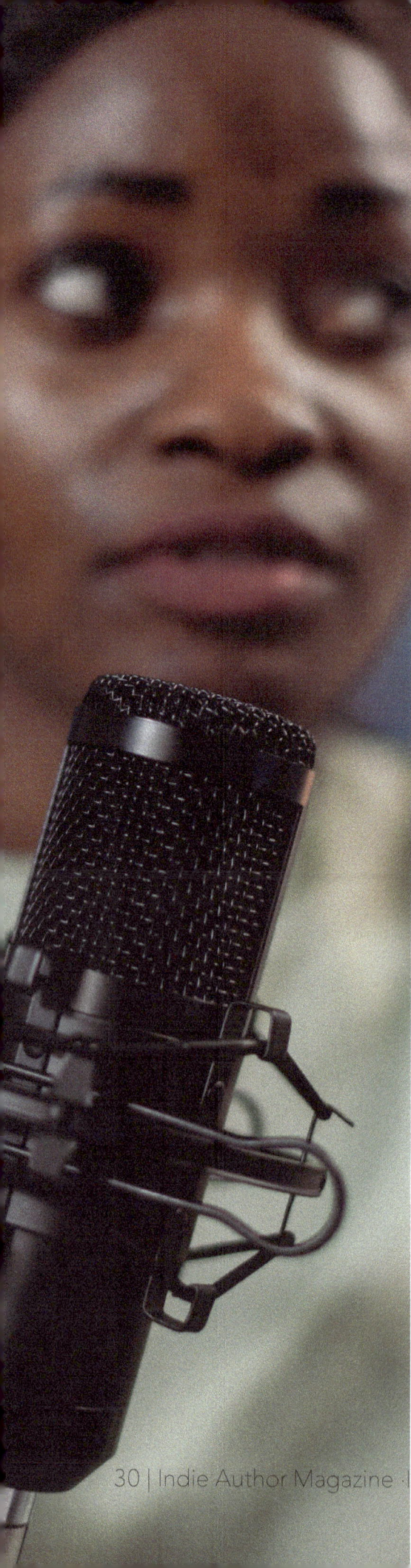

Setting the Stage

HOW YOU CAN PREPARE YOUR MANUSCRIPT FOR AUDIO NARRATION

You've selected your narrator or narrators, agreed to all the technical aspects of an audiobook project, and signed the contract to turn your words into an audio story for your listeners. Now what?

Despite what it may seem, even if it's already published as a paperback or e-book, your manuscript may still need some work to get it ready for audio, according to voice actors.

When exploring audiobook formats for their work, many authors choose to use the completed manuscript as is. In this case, the original manuscript is exactly what you'll hear in the audiobook. Others may make small changes to descriptions or dialogue in the story to make it fit the audio format better. Either way, taking a few extra steps at the start of any audio project to prepare your book can help you get the product you envision from the start and make the process run smoother for both author and narrator.

PASS YOUR NARRATOR A NOTE

Even if you choose not to edit your manuscript's content before recording an audiobook, providing your narrator with cues and notes beforehand can make their work easier and limit the need for corrections down the road. "Character description and name pronunciation is a plus," says voice actor Amy Strong. For example, you could include a thorough pronunciation guide, especially for anything made up or words that you want pronounced in a non-standard way. Narrator and producer J.S. Arquin adds, "Pronunciation guides are extremely helpful and appreciated. If you're a Fantasy or Sci-Fi author and don't know/don't care how all of your made-up things are pronounced and want to give your narrator free rein, that is fine too. Those of us who work in those genres deal with that a lot and can handle it, no problem. But if you're particular, definitely provide a pronunciation guide."

Author Alex R. Crawford provides her narrators with links to recorded pronunciations when they are available. She also includes a list of characters and accents. "If in a series, I will refer back to where they had spoken in a previous book. Additionally, my narrator keeps a sound file of voices used." This helps with continuity along more than one book and prompts listeners to understand who is speaking.

Another way to aid your narrator in bringing your world to life is to give them key insights into major characters. Author and narrator Elise Hoffman says, "Having a character list is really helpful—knowing which characters are important to that specific book or will be important in the future if it's a series [and] having a general passing knowledge of their attitude or events that would influence how the author wants them to be presented." She says giving your narrator advance notice of important or surprising events in the story may also be warranted. "Sometimes—but not always—a heads-up about big events that are system-shockers are good to know. I've, more than once, come upon a character death and been shell-shocked. Which can be good! It can definitely work, but if you want your narrator to know, tell them." Otherwise, she says, the author may get some surprised messages mid-project from the narrator who got invested in the story.

Notes on future plot points in a series or a character's planned arc can also save your narrator from undue stress as they are making up the voice or accents they will use. If, in one book, a narrator chooses a very difficult voice for a minor character, they are likely not going to be happy if that character is a major part of the next book. Some narrators, like author and narrator Cindy Gunderson, provide their own character sheet for background, pronunciation, and accent for authors to fill out. Crawford has another unique method for providing her narrator with feedback as she's recording. "My narrator records live on social media," Crawford says. "I'm able to watch/listen in, offering her the opportunity to ask a question, or me to provide instant feedback if there is a typo … or if there is a particularly difficult pronunciation … or any number of things."

AUDIO-FRIENDLY MANUSCRIPTS

Reading in your head and reading out loud are very different. If you have the ability, reading your prose out loud can identify repetitive or tricky phrases, such as the "soldier's shoulders shuddered" or "too close to close the clothes hamper." Your narrator can probably do it, but making small tweaks to your wording in certain passages can improve the recording in an audiobook. This process can also help you catch long, convoluted sentences that don't allow for easy breathing or flow. If you can make small changes, such as removing alliteration and shortening and simplifying longer sentences, you can get your book into great audiobook shape by simply reading it out loud yourself.

Another option is audio-first writing—writing the manuscript specifically for audio as a primary format. A blend of traditional novel writing and script writing, audio-first books might avoid dialogue tags with adjectives that could be given in the performance, such as "she said angrily" or "he whispered." Your narrator's voice could easily convey that, so having the words as well doesn't add much to the audio. Punctuation can also provide breathing room in the narration.

In addition, audio-first books allow the author to think about what they might show readers in a text format, like internal thoughts in italics, and how to translate those into audio, such as by muting the voice somewhat or adding another effect to differentiate between internal and external dialogue. When reading, paragraph breaks visually cue the reader that a new person is talking. Audio-first writers can move the attribution before the dialogue to indicate who is talking and help the listener know who is speaking. They can also focus on making dialogue cues more stage-direction-oriented instead of using the attribution "he said."

Writing for audio first can also allow for easy adaptation into duet-style narration, when two narrators each read a major character in the same production, or full-cast narration, when several narrators portray individual characters rather than one narrator using different voices for each. Duet narration is especially popular in Romance, particularly when a scene or chapter is told from one perspective before switching to the other main character perspective for the next scene or chapter.

A full-cast audiobook could include many narrators and sometimes even sound effects, bringing to mind the radio shows of decades past. Perusing the audiobook bestseller lists, full-cast audiobooks are selling well in many genres. Full-cast audiobooks are likely to be more of a script in format and may require significant revisions if the story is not written for audio first. But some full-cast audiobooks are being produced for popular books alongside a single-narrator version, enabling audiobook fans to choose how they want to engage with the story.

TIP-TOP TEXT

Once your audiobook manuscript's content is prepared and your notes for the narrator compiled, it's easy to format the text. "We usually record from a PDF, but delivery format doesn't matter that much, as everything is easily convertible," Arquin says. While some narrators may choose to highlight, mark in breathing points, or take notes, others simply read through the book. Ensuring adequate time according to your narrator's needs will allow for sufficient preparation.

Whether you are using your manuscript as is, adjusting a manuscript with small edits, or writing for audio first, listen to your audiobook narrator to find out what steps you can take as the author to make the process run smoothly. Together, you can polish that audiobook project and really make it shine. ■

Jen B. Green

Jen B Green

Jen B. Green has lived in five countries on four continents with her three sons, two daughters, and one great guy. She reads anything that stays still long enough, plays piano, and bakes everything sweet.

After earning her Ph.D. in psychology, Jen tried writing a novel for Nanowrimo and was hooked! Her days are spent traveling the world, teaching undergraduate psychology, and wrangling her growing homemade army, but her nights are for writing Urban Fantasy with witches and werewolves.

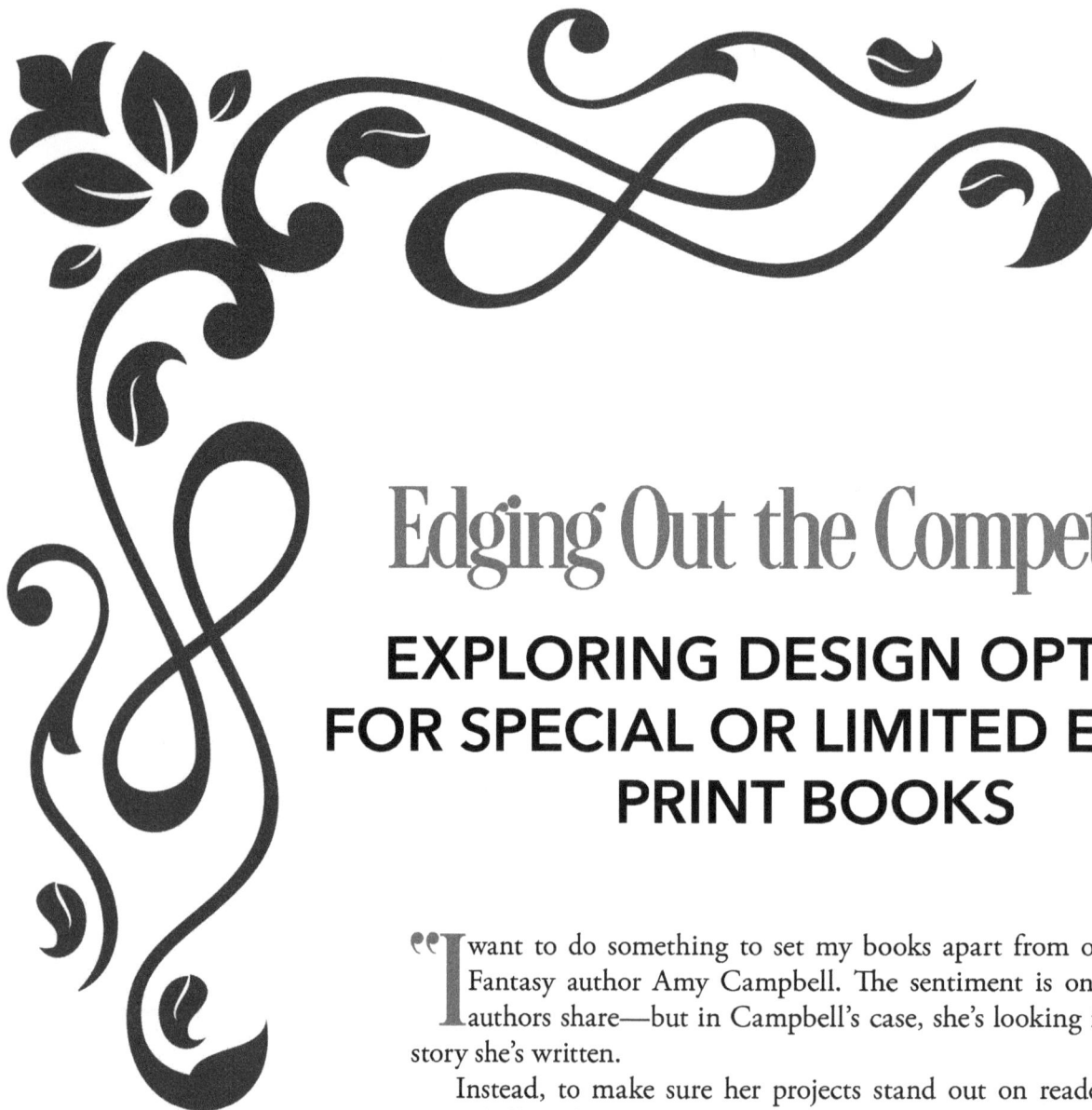

Edging Out the Competition

EXPLORING DESIGN OPTIONS FOR SPECIAL OR LIMITED EDITION PRINT BOOKS

"I want to do something to set my books apart from others," says Fantasy author Amy Campbell. The sentiment is one plenty of authors share—but in Campbell's case, she's looking far past the story she's written.

Instead, to make sure her projects stand out on readers' shelves, Campbell explores special edition design options for her print books. For her next book, Campbell has chosen to hire an artist to do sprayed edges after struggling to do it herself in the past; she ruled out fore-edge designs when she chose a full-bleed option for interior artwork. After running three successful Kickstarter campaigns for special editions, Campbell says she's come to the conclusion authors who want to provide readers with extra design elements in their books should "either be ready to learn new skill sets or hire people who can do the things you can't," she says.

Both choices tend to require money and time away from working on new manuscripts, so most authors limit fancy design options to special editions, where they can focus on presentation rather than content. But with such a range of creative options at varying price points, the decision of what design elements to include in a special edition is anything but limited. "Generally, the folks purchasing these special editions have already read the books in digital form, so the text itself isn't the most important factor," says Dark Romance author Samantha Rue. "Readers are buying it for the way it enhances their immersion into the story, universe, and characters."

If you're ready to explore specialized design options for your book, first consider whether you intend them for the e-book, paperback, or hardback edition, as some limitations may apply. "There are so many ways to make a book a special edition; there's no one definition of a special edition," says YA Fantasy author Liz Delton. "How you end up making your book special, be it new cover design or color illustrations or sprayed edges, is really up to you."

The following design options are primarily recommended for paperback or hardback books. Cost will vary depending on the complexity of the design, how much of it you can do yourself, and who you choose to work with for each step of the production process.

FORMATTING DESIGN OPTIONS

Some specialty design options can be added to your manuscript's design file before it goes to the printer, whether that's through a print-on-demand service or a traditional bulk print run. Because of that, you might do some of them yourself, depending on your level of comfort with formatting programs, or you may be able to hire a professional formatter to add these elements for you. Design elements incorporated into the interior formatting of a book can be part of a special edition, but these options are flexible; because they're part of the book's print file and work via print-on-demand services, they can also help your standard paperbacks stand out from the crowd.

CHAPTER HEADER IMAGES

Chapter header images can be full-page, full-color images printed under the text of the first page, or initial spread, of a chapter, or they can be simpler, black-and-white designs that cover the top quarter of a page. Chapter header designs can also include small images that incorporate the chapter number without taking up much extra space on the page. Author and graphic designer K. Iwancio says, "My readers love the chapter art. It makes any black-and-white book that much more fancy."

Images on this page courtesy of Mallory Rock
of Rock Solid Book Design
www.RockSolidBookDesign.com

For authors who prefer a DIY approach, chapter headers are probably the easiest way for you to add design details to your book. You can purchase art with the appropriate licensing, or create your own designs using tools like Canva, Affinity, or Photoshop, then add them into your manuscript file during formatting.

Pro Tip: Remember to choose images with high contrast if you stick with black-and-white images. Subtle color shifts tend to blur together if the tones are too close.

"I used two-page chapter images in my Thriller, one for each of the two POV characters, to mark their chapters," says multi-genre author Erica Damon. "I love the look of it, and many readers have agreed it's a fun detail for the paperback. I love watching folks flip through it at vendor events. However, it did make formatting harder as all the chapters had to end on right-side pages so that there were no awkward blanks." Damon says she's also included chapter header images in her Romance books to differentiate who's narrating the chapter. "I write a lot of multi- or dual POV, so it's a fun way for me to get a little extra about marking which character the chapter will be told by."

Choosing artwork for your chapter headers can be difficult, but there are many ways to gather designs: run a contest; purchase from Etsy; or hire an artist through Fivrr, Upwork, or Deviant Art. Some authors also create their own art using AI programs such as MidJourney or DALL-E.

If you choose to format your headers yourself, check out online tutorials like T.A. Hernandez's "Book Formatting in Word," or try one of these formatting tools: Atticus, Vellum, or Adobe InDesign. Otherwise, hire a specialist, like Serendipity Formatting by Erica Alexander (https://ericaalexander.wixsite.com/formats/gallery).

FORE-EDGE DESIGN

Fore-edge design, a relatively newer design option, is the digital response to sprayed edges. Instead of painting directly on the edge of a completed book, fore-edge design is incorporated into the formatting of a book, printed in the tiny space of the page margins, up against where the page gets cut. Because the

Images on this page courtesy of www.KingdomCovers.com
Images on the facing page found on Barnes&Noble

design is printed on the face of the page, it shows best and brightest when the book is open and the pages fan out to either side. Individual pages will show dots and dashes along the edge that only resolve into a complete image when the pages are fanned in a cascade. But since the inked design sits against the edge of the facing pages, the bleed will show through when the book is closed, giving the illusion of a sprayed-edge design.

Fore-edge designs can be applied to all three sides of a page, but the top and bottom edges will not have the impressive cascading effect when the book opens, since the pages only fan out to either side. That said, some designers use the top to create built-in tabs readers can use to identify different sections of the book, like alternate POVs or multiple volumes bound together.

Because fore-edge designs are a newer feature, few formatters currently offer the service, so authors may need to plan ahead to find a formatter who's able to create the design element. Adding color increases the cost of printing, but if you choose a black-and-white design, fore-edge designs can be added to a PDF of your manuscript during the last phase of formatting without increasing printing fees.

A couple companies currently offering fore-edge design services include Painted Wings Publishing (https://www.paintedwingspublishing.com/) and Kingdom Covers (https://kingdomcovers.com/fore-edge-design/). Kingdom Covers is the design company owned by *IAM* Creative Director Alice Briggs.

POST-PRODUCTION DESIGN OPTIONS

Beyond the design elements authors can add before a book goes to print, there are several post-production options that can be applied to a book after printing, or as part of the printing process for hardcover books. Because of the level of specialized skill and the time required to do these well, most authors who go this route will want to hire an artist or contract out the work. Since they require a bulk print order instead of print-on-demand and can be more costly, post-production design options are popular with special edition crowdfunding campaigns.

SPRAYED EDGES

More commonly used for special editions, Kickstarter campaigns, and rewards tiers, sprayed edges turn a printed book into a work of art. Unlike fore-edge designs, which are added to the formatting of a book before it is printed, sprayed edges are painted onto the book after printing. The design, whether it's a solid color or stenciled artwork, is applied to the closed edges of a book. So while fore-edge designs depend on the ink bleeding through to show on the closed edge, sprayed edges have a more saturated color when the book is closed. There may be some bleed-through on the interior of the pages, but it's likely to be smaller and more irregular than the engineered marks left by fore-edge designs.

Sprayed edges can be harder for an author to DIY, as doing so requires more space for storage and

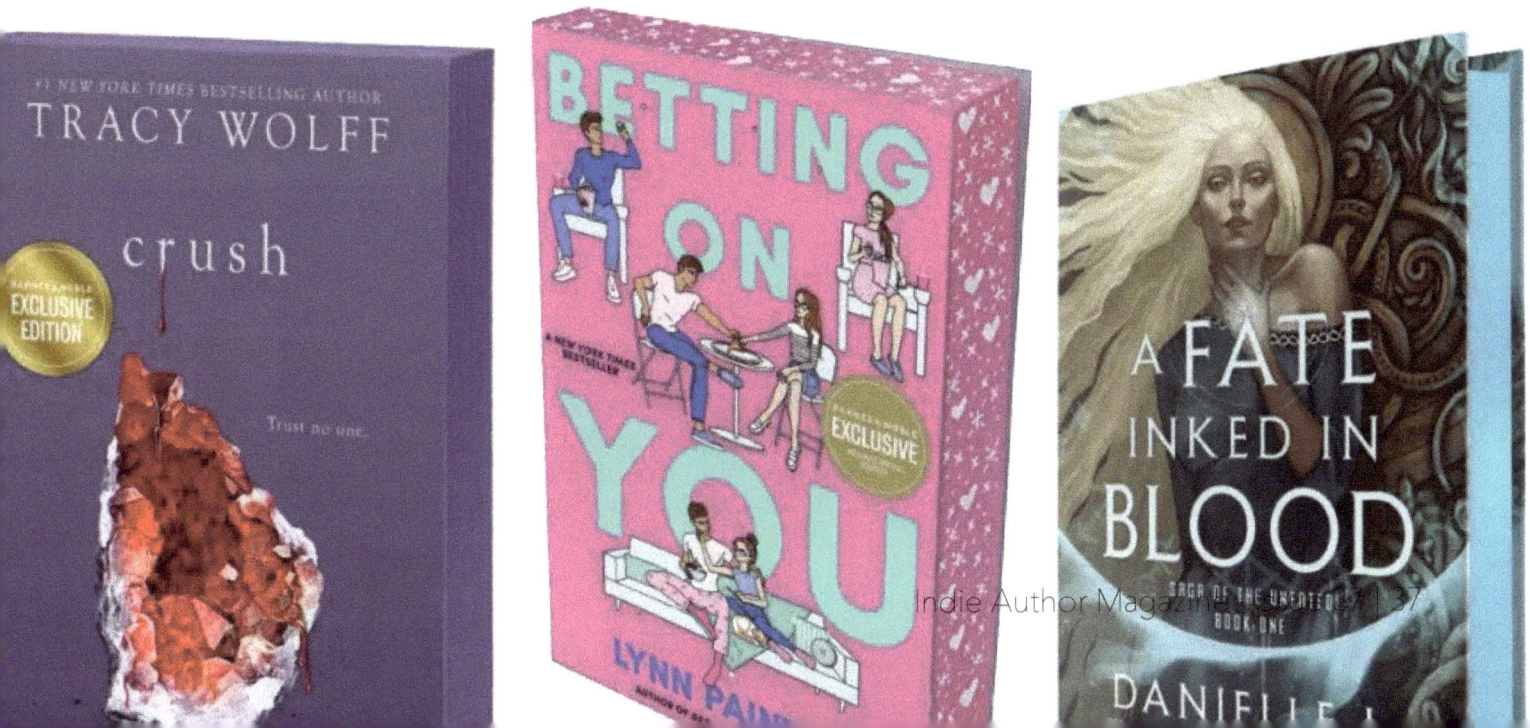

tools. Books must be clamped to hold the pages tightly during painting, and covers must be protected from both the pressure of the clamps and any stray paint. Kayla of @KaysHiddenShelf recently broke down her process for trying to develop a cost-effective method in a video titled "How to Spray Book Edges at Home" on her YouTube channel.

FOILED COVERS

Foiled books catch the light and readers' eyes. The metallic detail is perfect for a print run of special editions, but since foil can be applied to the front cover as a 3D or stamped finish, you can use this effect on either hardbacks or paperbacks. Foil also makes for fun shiny edges, and as Rue says, "Let's face it, we're all secretly crows attracted to shiny things."

Authors can order foil-stamping through several independent printing companies. With 48 Hour Books, the process only adds four days to the regular print order turnaround, according to the printer's website. Print Ninja and Presto Page also offer foil-stamping services.

CHOOSE YOUR DESIGN

The upgrades don't stop here. Whether you're developing a special edition or just want your book to stand out, other options to consider include details like faux leather covers, colored endpapers, world maps, or ribbon bookmarks. As with most publishing decisions, choosing which design elements work best for your book will take balance: time, money, skills, and your own network of resources. ◼

Jenn Lessmann

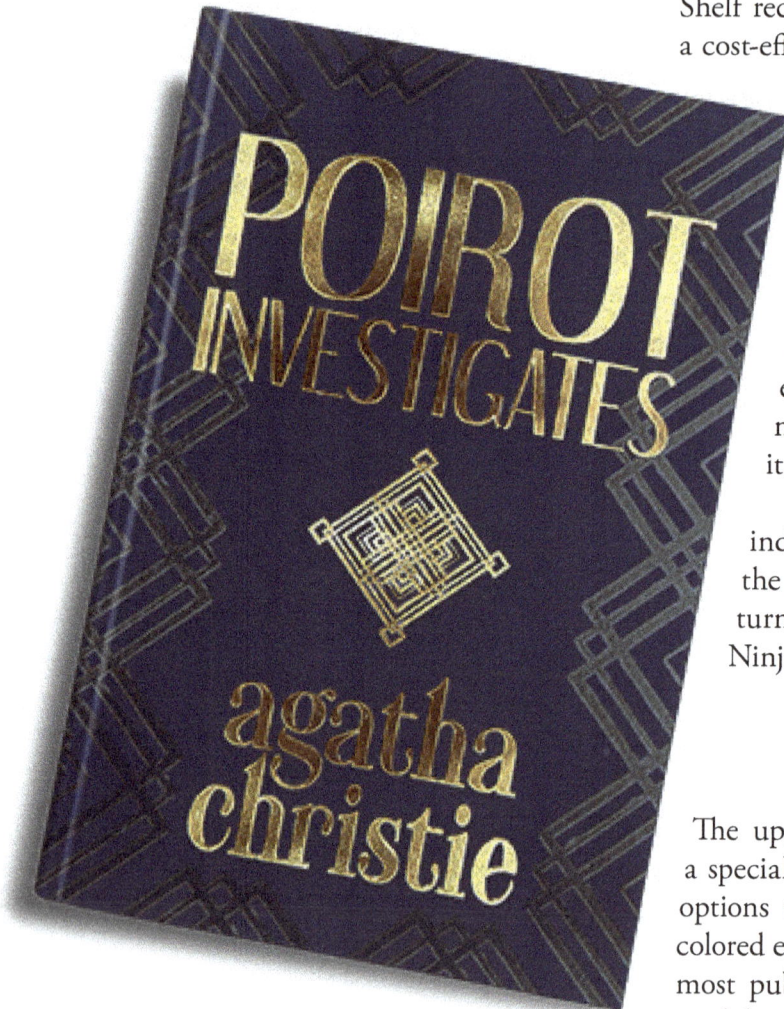

Image courtesy of www.KingdomCovers.com

Jenn Lessmann

Jenn Lessmann is the author of Unmagical: a Witchy Mystery and three stories on Kindle Vella. A former barista, stage manager, and high school English teacher with advanced degrees from impressive colleges, she continues to drink excessive amounts of caffeine, stay up later than is absolutely necessary, and read three or four books at a time. Jenn is currently studying witchcraft and the craft of writing, and giggling internally whenever they intersect. She writes snarky paranormal fantasy for new adults whenever her dog will allow it.

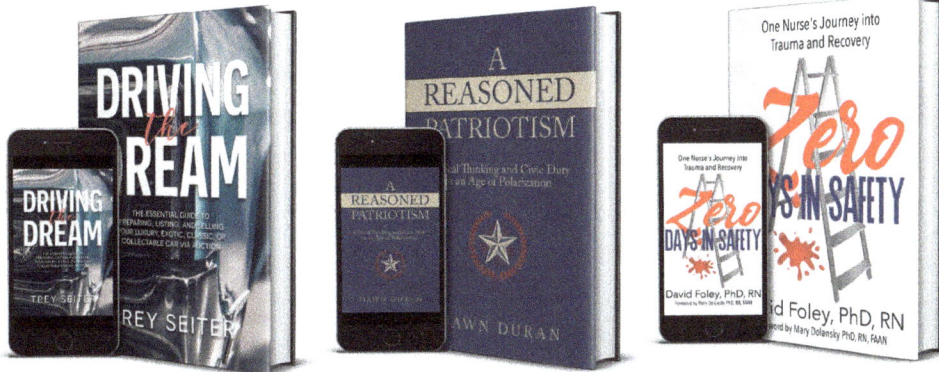

Craft Consistency with a Style Bible for Book Formatting

Book formatting lays the cornerstone for captivating your readers from the very first glance. Beyond aesthetics, it plays a crucial role in enhancing the reader experience and establishing the credibility of your work. Meticulousness and attention to detail are necessary during the writing, marketing, and production stages, especially considering the wide variety of software platforms and devices on which books are provided. In paperback or hardcover editions, consistent formatting invites your readers to better immerse themselves in the text; in electronic formats, especially with reflowable EPUBs that allow readers to alter font and text size, it can make a sizable impact on the story's aesthetic presence and readability.

Keeping track of your formatting preferences in a central location not only aids in your consistency and organizational skills but also reduces stress during the production process. Additionally, failing to communicate when submitting your manuscript to a typesetter increases the likelihood that they will make changes that do not align with your intended vision. This type of misunderstanding can delay the production timeline and potentially introduce inconsistencies to the manuscript as well as added expenses during the editing process.

Should you choose to format your book or work with a typesetter, a style bible may help with maintaining formatting consistency. A style bible is a comprehensive guide outlining your manuscript's formatting preferences and guidelines. Just as your editor may work with you to create editorial style guides that specify punctuation rules or unique spellings for your series, a formatting style bible can benefit both authors and publishing team members by serving as a reference for maintaining coherence in formatting.

UNDERSTANDING FORMATTING CHALLENGES

Before we delve into the creation of your style bible, it's essential to understand the common formatting challenges that authors face. Something as simple as minor inconsistencies across platforms or misinterpreting formatting can disrupt the reading experience and complicate your production process.

I've experienced these challenges firsthand while working with a typesetter. While creating my manuscript, I used automatic formatting features such as hard indentations using the tab key in the Word document. Unfortunately, the features failed to translate into Atticus, the formatting software that my typesetter used. All the formatting was altered, creating more work on her end. Needless to say, she was not very happy with me, and I felt frustrated by the need to extend my release date.

Formatting loss disrupts the author's vision and adds unnecessary time and effort to the production process at best. At worst, it can create issues with the readability of a published book that's already in readers' hands. When it comes to overcoming these challenges, establishing and adhering to clear formatting guidelines throughout the manuscript can allow for a smoother transition from manuscript to published work, whether you're producing a paperback, hardback, or reflowable EPUB.

CREATING A STYLE BIBLE

A style bible is a centralized repository that offers numerous benefits for authors and publishing teams alike.

Consistency: A style bible ensures consistency in formatting throughout the manuscript, including font styles, sizes, spacing, and indentation.

Efficiency: By providing clear guidelines and instructions for formatting, a style bible streamlines the editing and typesetting process. Authors and publishing teams can save time and effort by referring to the style bible for guidance, reducing the need for manual adjustments and revisions.

Communication: A style bible serves as a communication tool between authors, editors, and typesetters, so production team members understand all formatting preferences, minimizing the risk of errors or inconsistencies.

Continuity: Authors can customize the style bible to uphold their individual aesthetic and publishing goals across the scope of their book series.

Adaptability: As manuscripts may undergo revisions or be formatted for different publishing formats (e.g., e-books, print books), a style bible provides a consistent reference point for adapting formatting across various platforms. Authors can easily update their style bible as needed to accommodate changes or new formatting requirements.

Professionalism: Utilizing a style bible demonstrates to the publishing professionals on your team a commitment to professionalism and attention to detail in the publishing process.

Establishing your paragraph and character styles provides uniformity in your font style, font size, and spacing. Differentiating between character formatting and paragraph styles is crucial for maintaining consistency across platforms. Similarly, when you create a guideline for these components, it creates a cohesive reading experience.

Basic elements to consider including in your style bible include

- Preferred fonts and styles.
- Paragraph and line spacing: This includes setting your line height, spacing before and after paragraphs, and indentations.
- Chapter headings and subheadings: You will want to format your chapter headings and subheadings to differentiate sections within your manuscript. This includes drop caps, font styles, sizes, alignment, and spacing for headings.
- Block quotes and pull quotes: Both Atticus and Vellum support formatting for block quotes and pull quotes, which can be especially useful for nonfiction authors. Customization of block quotes, including indentation, font styles, and alignment, will distinguish them from regular text, and consistent formatting can indicate to the reader the information they'll find in those sections.
- Lists and bullet points: You can create bulleted and numbered lists within your manuscript, including customization options for bullet styles, indentation, and spacing.
- Page layout and margin customizations, taking into consideration page size and orientation depending on the print dimensions you choose.
- E-book and print formatting: For e-book and print publication, you can generate e-book files in various formats, such as EPUB, DOC or DOCX, or PDF, and print-ready PDF files suitable for publication.

DETAILS MATTER

Once you've decided on formatting basics for your book, here are a few additional formatting elements that you may want to include in your style bible:

Paragraph Indentation

- Specify the preferred indentation for the first line of paragraphs, such as a standard 0.5 inches. According to the Chicago Manual of Style, the standard style guide for fiction writing, the first paragraph in a chapter or other section within a manuscript normally begins flush left, and only subsequent paragraphs are indented by half an inch. This is a convention more than a rule, but most publishers today, including Chicago Manual of Style, tend to follow it. When formatting for print, the standard indent is about half that.
- Apply indentations through paragraph formatting options in your word processor, as tab indents do not carry over into KDP.
- When stating the indentation method in your style bible, provide clear instructions along with examples to illustrate the desired formatting. Additionally, consider including screenshots or step-by-step instructions for applying your preferred indentation settings. This will help editors and typesetters accurately implement the preferred indentation style throughout the manuscript.

Bulleted Lists

- Provide specific instructions on the preferred bullet style, indentation, spacing, and alignment for bulleted lists in different sections of the manuscript.

Headers and Subheadings

- Establish a clear hierarchical structure and formatting consistency for headers and subheads to guide readers through the content effectively.
- Outline the hierarchy of headers/subheads; specify the font style, size, spacing, and alignment for each level; and provide examples of their usage.

Block Quotes

- Maintain consistent formatting and indentation for block quotes to distinguish them from regular text and highlight important excerpts.
- Define the formatting for block quotes, including indentation, and specify when and how they should be used within the manuscript.

Spacing

- Ensure margins, line spacing, and indentation are consistent throughout the manuscript to create a polished and professional appearance.
- Provide guidelines for setting margins, line spacing, paragraph indentation, and spacing between headings, paragraphs, and lists.

Smart versus Straight Quotation Marks

- Smart quotes are quotation marks that curl toward the text they're surrounding whereas straight quotes appear the same whether they're at the beginning or end of a quote. Use smart quotes, and smart apostrophes, for a typographically correct and visually appealing presentation, ensuring uniformity across the manuscript.
- In your style bible, specify the preference for smart quotes over straight quotes, along with instructions on enabling smart quotes in word processing software and guidelines for maintaining consistency in their usage.

Pro Tip: When using Word's advanced "Find and Replace" setting and with "Use Wildcards" checked, the codes ^34 and ^39 will identify any straight quotation marks and straight apostrophes, respectively, in your document.

Incorporating these elements into your style bible can help ensure consistency and coherence in the final manuscript when communicating your formatting preferences to editors and typesetters.

You can curate a seamless publishing journey by taking charge and simplifying your production process or your collaboration with an editor and typesetter with a well-designed style bible. This will provide a smoother production experience for you or your publishing team and could even save you time and money. A well-crafted style bible isn't just another tool in a writer's arsenal—it's the passport to a smoother, stress-free journey from manuscript to masterpiece. ■

Eryka Parker

Eryka Parker

Eryka Parker is a book coach, an award-winning developmental editor, and writing instructor. As a women's contemporary author under the pen name Zariah L. Banks, she creates emotional intimacy novels that prove that everyone deserves to feel seen, appreciated, and loved. She lives in Northeast Ohio with her husband and two children and is currently working on her third novel.

An Answer to AI Audiobook Debates?

SOUNDED WALKS THE ETHICAL TIGHTROPE OF AI NARRATION

The intersection of artificial intelligence and the realm of audiobook narration has ushered in a wave of innovation, but it also brings with it a host of ethical considerations that demand careful examination. As the capabilities of AI voice cloning evolve, the ethical landscape of replicating the voices of audiobook narrators has become a focal point of discussion.

One primary concern revolves around the potential impact on the livelihoods of human narrators. The advent of AI voice cloning poses the question whether automating narration with synthetic voices could diminish opportunities for human narrators in the audiobook industry. Striking a balance between technological advancement and safeguarding employment opportunities within creative fields is a complex ethical minefield.

However, a new audiobook platform, Sounded, hopes its unique approach to the projects will allow it to dance through that minefield unscathed.

We met with Sounded's Chief Legal Officer Jason Kelly to learn about the new platform and to talk ethics around AI audiobook narration.

WHAT IS SOUNDED?

Sounded (https://authors.sounded.com) is a real-time audiobook production platform, principally for self-published authors and smaller publishing houses, that allows authors or publishers to create an audiobook in real time. Users have a choice of over 824 narrators that are available across sixty languages and 162 dialects. But Sounded is also attempting to balance the scales for narrators by offering a service with real voice artists through a program called True Voice.

"We work directly with narrators to create a digital replica, which is effectively a digital version of their vocal characteristics," Kelly says. "We license the vocal characteristics from the narrator or voice artist with consent. Any audiobook projects that are narrated using the digital replica are also consented to by the voice artist or narrator. For example, they may not want their voice to be associated with Spicy Romance, or there could be a political connotation that they're not happy about. They have control and can say 'yes' or 'no' [to a project]. Outside of that, what's very, very important is that the voice artist also receives a commission, even though it's a digital replica that's being used for narration. And again, we're here to work with technology in a responsible manner and work with voice artists to produce the best audiobooks that we can."

Building a regulated business model is important to Sounded, Kelly explains. "We work on a model of what's known as three C's, which is consent, control, and commission," he says. "As we've built a technology-based platform, we've always respected intellectual property rights. We've ensured that we don't use, and haven't taken, any copyrighted text into our platform. We've also never taken in any audio files or samples from the public domain. As we produce audiobooks with the digital replicas on the platform, the voice artist also has control over the process. They get to decide whether they want their vocal characteristics and digital replica associated with a particular text."

Kelly believes that the business model of the three C's works across all AI tech business companies. "Anyone creating an AI product with consent, control, and commission is building a business with a good foundation," he says.

WHAT DOES IT COST?

Sounded has three levels of membership: the basic tier at $99, the exclusive tier at $249, and the elite tier at $999. At the basic tier, users can select from all 824 narrators. This membership tier allows you to produce an audiobook and distribute it on the platform exclusively for three years, where you set the price point. Additionally, you can offer it for sale in any region you choose. The author receives a royalty payment of 40 percent per sale.

The exclusive tier requires one-year exclusivity with Sounded for the distribution of the audiobook itself but has a 60 percent return to the author or publisher. However, the highest tier, labeled "elite," allows authors to take audiobook files straight from the platform and distribute them on other platforms. If distributing the audiobook through Sounded, elite users receive a royalty return of 80 percent on a non-exclusive basis. The elite tier also has access to the True Voice platform, meaning users can engage the services of a real voice artist whose digital replica is available on the platform.

HOW CAN AI AUDIOBOOKS BE MADE WITH ETHICS IN MIND?

As with other areas of the publishing world, the advent of AI-narrated audiobooks in recent years have raised plenty of concern. Narrators have pushed back against the use of their voices without their consent to train and produce artificially generated works, especially in cases where the projects may include adult content. On the other hand, authors in support of AI have emphasized the lower cost and ease of production of AI audiobooks, and all big five distributors—Apple Books, Barnes & Noble, Google Play, Kobo, and Amazon—now allow for their creation and/or distribution.

Kelly says one of the biggest areas of debate relates to narrators' consent to their voices being used for a project. "You have to think of levels of consent. If somebody loses mental capacity at some point, they're no longer able to consent. Equally, if they're deceased, they're no longer able to consent." As a result, Sounded ensures within its contract all digital replicas on the platform are from narrators who can consent to the use of their voice within their contract, and generated voices on Sounded's platform are trained only on copyright-expired work.

"There's businesses out there that have different models around ethics and how that works," Kelly says. "But as a business, we've decided to adopt that particular approach based on

advice we've received and also our current beliefs on how to adopt a sensible, regulated position and business model."

WHAT'S NEXT FOR THE PLATFORM?

Sounded launched only a year ago, in April 2023, but Kelly says the program already has new features in the works. "We have a feature called Multicharacter coming later in 2024. It will allow any author to select multiple voices within a book. If you have a novel with many speaking parts, you can have different voices assigned to those speaking parts in the book. The enhanced true voice products are not available right now as a self-service basis, but we have a number of voice artists that we have those digital replicas licensed for. They will all be added to our platform during 2024."

If you're interested in finding out more about Sounded, the company will present at the London Stories Festival in September, Frankfurt Book Fair in October, and at book fairs in Bologna and Madrid, or you can contact them at info@sounded.com. ∎

Elaine Bateman

Elaine Bateman

In her pre-author life, Elaine worked for FTSE 100 and Fortune 500 companies in procurement, project support, and IT Training. She has a bachelor of science. in Systems Practice and Design.

From the Stacks

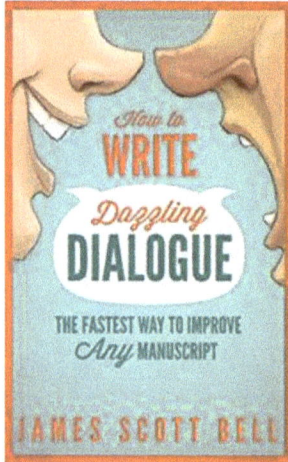

How to Write Dazzling Dialogue by James Scott Bell
https://books2read.com/u/47xd8N

It never hurts to brush up on the basics, and even if your book's dialogue is great, like with any creative writing skill, it can always be made better. *How to Write Dazzling Dialogue: The Fastest Way to Improve Any Manuscript* compiles lectures from author and writing coach James Scott Bell's writing seminars to explore what makes dialogue memorable in fiction and teach you how to improve your own.

Audacity
https://audacityteam.org

For authors exploring ways to record and edit their own audio for audiobooks, podcasts, or transmedia opportunities, Audacity is free, professional-quality editing software with a relatively small learning curve. Users can record directly in the program or import audio files, as well as improve the audio quality with options to reduce noise, re-record sections of audio, or add effects. Finished projects can be exported in several common file types, including MP3 and WAV, with the help of a free plugin.

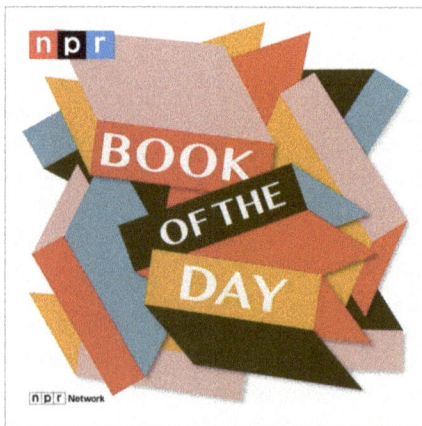

NPR's Book of the Day
https://npr.org/podcasts/510364/daily-books

Every writer should also be a reader, but if you've hit a slump, NPR's reader-focused podcast may be the answer. In bite-sized episodes around fifteen minutes or less, *NPR's Book of the Day* sums up a different book each weekday, covering a range of genres and writing styles. There are suggestions for nearly every reader, "whether you're looking to engage with the big questions of our times—or temporarily escape from them," according to NPR's website. (And don't forget to search for any reader-focused podcasts specific to your genre to learn what's piquing your audience's interest!)

" The Magic of Disappearing Dialogue Tags

BEST PRACTICES FOR WRITING AND FORMATTING DIALOGUE

" Ah, the humble dialogue tag. They are some of the most powerful tools in your author toolbox, helping your reader visualize a scene and who's speaking, and often conveying subtle action. But despite their value in a story, they're best when they're not even noticed.

Many writers, both inexperienced and seasoned, stumble over how to best utilize dialogue tags.

"Let's look at dialogue tags," she said. And so we shall.

DIALOGUE TAGS: SEEN BUT NOT HEARD

When writing third-person point-of-view stories, using the basic tag "said"—or "says" for present tense, and "asked" and "replied" for questions and responses—is one of the best things you can use in your novels.

Although the word "said" is about as exciting and descriptive as the color beige, you might be surprised how effective it is. Generally, readers like lots of dialogue tags, especially when there are rapid-fire conversations or more than two people speaking. Using simple words makes dialogue tags invisible to the reader.

The rule is a bit looser for first-person or close third-person narratives. Depending on how you're telling the story, and how you handle dialogue, your tags may end up being internalized or less formal, reflecting the narrator's voice.

For all points of view, qualify the tone once in a while using a word like "whispered" or "chortled," particularly when you want to make a point. But use such words sparingly. Dialogue tags are best when seen but not heard, and the more your protagonist guffaws, whines, and hisses, the more likely you'll make your reader groan.

THE ADVERB CONUNDRUM

In his book *On Writing,* Stephen King famously advises people to avoid adverbs at all costs. While writers everywhere debate the point, when it comes to dialogue tags, King was absolutely correct. Over one hundred years ago, Tom Swift novels used adverbs to modify "said" or other verbs within dialogue tags. For example:

"Don't go over there," he cried worriedly.
"I won't," she called back, cheerfully.

Using adverbs in this way will muddy your prose, and many writers consider it a lazy way to describe the actual conversation.

Rather than resort to adverbs, there's a better solution. Embed character actions into your dialogue tags. This will enrich the scene and make your characters more lifelike. Try something like this instead.

His eyes went wide, and he ran in her direction. "Don't go over there!"

"I won't." Janey dropped into the grass yards away from the fence where the dog was barking and started picking dandelions.

By adding descriptive actions, you can avoid dialogue tags entirely while better conveying the setting, character's mood, or physical actions.

THE PUNCTUATION PUZZLE

When writing dialogue and associated tags in American English, enclose the spoken words within double quotation marks, with the comma, period, or question mark inside the quotation marks. And start a new paragraph each time the speaker changes.

For example:

"How are you?" she asked.
"Middling," he replied. "I've been better."

If a quote appears within another line of dialogue, alternate double quotation marks and single quotation marks as follows: "She said to tell you 'Happy birthday,'" I said. British English and other countries will place the terminal punctuation outside the quotes and may also utilize single quotation marks in place of double quotation marks, and vice versa.

DON'T BE AFRAID TO SPICE IT UP

As you write, practice variety. Here are some things to try:

- Vary the location of dialogue tags, sometimes using them at the start of a sentence and sometimes at the end.
- Break up the first sentence in a longer speech with a dialogue tag. For example: "When I was a boy," Lincoln said, removing his hat and wiping his forehead, "life was a lot easier than it is today."
- Write rapid conversations, such as when people are angry or scared, with minimal tags, and see how it changes the pacing.
- Play around with interruptions. For example, "But I thought you said—" he began, only to be cut off by her sharp retort, "I don't care what you thought!"

Truly skilled authors will use dialogue tags so masterfully that they bring the dialogue to life with an economy of words, allowing the reader to visualize the entire scene without getting distracted by the little cues along the way. ■

Jackie Dana

Jackie Dana

Jackie had a few practice careers before finally deciding to become a full-time writer. To keep the computer humming and her cats fed, she's a freelance writer and editor. She's also the brains behind Story Cauldron, a Substack newsletter devoted to storytelling and the writing process as well as the home of her current YA novel series, The Favor Faeries.

PROSPERITY

More Formats, More Options, More Money

Following this month's theme on formats, I thought I'd share the change of heart—and mind—I had about the formats in which I opt to publish my books.

When I first started publishing, e-books were the hot new thing. It was an option Amazon offered—"Would you like us to publish the e-book to accompany your print book?"—as I was listing my first book for sale.

Imagine my delight a few years later when I realized my e-book income was quite substantial. I thought, "Oh, I'll just publish e-books." I'd heard print was dead, loved the idea of not having to publish a print version, and I was mostly reading on my new Kindle.

Only to come to a hard realization sometime later I wasn't supposed to publish in the format that worked best for me; I was supposed to publish in the format that works best for my reader.

Oops.

Turns out there was a solid business argument for publishing in every format possible: e-book, print, and audio. Having your books in all formats provides multiple streams of income from one book. One book published in different formats provides three or even four streams of income—and if you publish them "wide," or on multiple retail sites, you can double, triple, or even quadruple those streams.

In addition, it turns out there's a solid reader argument for publishing in every format possible.

Some readers prefer to have all of their books with them, so they can read whatever strikes their fancy, wherever they are. This is me.

Some readers prefer the look, feel, and read of a physical book because the story takes them away; they like the feel of an actual book; or they want to underline, highlight, and make notes as they read. This is also me.

Some readers like to listen to their books while they are working out, driving, or doing myriad other tasks. This is also me.

The format I prefer when I read depends on whether the book is fiction or nonfiction. It also depends on who the author is. Do we have a relationship? Will I want to post a photo to help with their marketing? I even consider whether the book will be one I want to read and re-read. (I'm looking at you, *Law of Success*.)

Some books I love so much, I buy them in every format.

Of course, on the author's side, we have to consider the cost of production in providing different formats to our readers. It can be an investment to produce a quality print book, and each version requires a certain type of file, and audiobooks must meet the standards of online platforms—another investment. I've written many articles about embracing a prosperity consciousness. Let me mention again how important it is to invest in your author business with the expectation you'll receive a many-multiple return on that investment. Consider adding different formats as you realize a return on the others.

Make sure your readers have every channel available to them to discover and read your book, which will be a force multiplier for your author business. You'll be so glad you did! ■

Honorée Corder

Honorée Corder

Honorée Corder is the author of more than fifty books, an empire builder, and encourager of writers. When she's not writing, she's spoiling her dog and two cats, eating something fabulous her husband made on the grill, working out, or reading. She hopes this article made a positive impact on your life, and if it did, you'll reach out to her via HonoreeCorder.com.

Two Birds, One Net Gain

HOW NATURE CAN IMPROVE YOUR HEALTH AND YOUR WRITING

If the longer, warmer, and sunnier days leading into summer don't lure you outside, away from your desk, this might entice you: going outside in nature is good for your mental and physical health, and for your writing.

As writers, the work we do is with our minds, not our bodies—unless we're enacting a fight scene to get those key details right. Writing is often solitary, and sedentary, work. But according to the Centers for Disease Control and Prevention, that physical inactivity can lead to long-term harm, including heart disease, type 2 diabetes, and cancer.

Engaging in physical activity out in nature is one way to soak up health benefits, such as better sleep, increased vitamin D production, improved energy and focus, and emotional and mental health restoration. Additionally, according to a 2022 study published by the National Center for Biotechnology Information, time spent in nature increases your creativity. The variety of health benefits going outside offers can directly benefit your writing work.

MIXING WORK AND PLEASURE

While you're outside, you can still work but in a different, relaxed, and meditative way. Nature offers a wealth of sensory experiences. Harness details from your time outside to infuse directly into your writing, bringing scenes alive so your readers more fully enter the worlds you create. What you see, hear, smell, touch, and taste can influence how you portray your characters and their interactions with their world.

Threading descriptive sensory details into your writing creates a more immersive experience for your readers by engaging their own senses, tapping directly into their brain through your words. For writers, vivid, bold imagery can paint your scenes into vibrant life. Taking the time for some activity out in nature can be a boon to your health and your writing endeavors.

WRITE OUTSIDE YOUR DOOR

Take advantage of your time outside by turning it into a writing exercise. After you've gotten some physical activity, find a spot where you can stand or sit comfortably. Remove your shoes and place your bare feet on the earth.

Once you're comfortable, close your eyes and take three slow, deep breaths, exhaling a little longer than the inhale.

Now, work through each of your senses:

Touch: Begin with the sensation of your feet on the ground. What are your toes and the soles of your feet experiencing? Is the ground cool or warm? Rough or gentle?

Smell: Inhale deeply. What scents do you detect: fresh-mown lawn, manure placed on a garden bed, a whiff of pine trees?

Hearing: Close your eyes and concentrate on as many sounds as your ears can capture. What do you hear? Birds? Insects? Traffic and machinery?

Sight: Open your eyes. What objects, shapes, and colors are around you?

Taste: You don't need to lick the bark of a tree for this one … unless you're so moved. Does the air have a taste? Is there a feeling of refreshment on your tongue?

Take a notebook to record your thoughts and impressions. Be wary of using a computer or your notes app, as you might become distracted with emails and scrolling, which defeats the purpose of your work outside. ∎

Desiree Smith-Daughety

Desiree Smith-Daughety

Desiree Smith-Daughety lives just a short paddle away from the Chesapeake Bay. She has been published in multiple publications, including Up.St.ART Annapolis magazine. Her home is in words and in the beauty and mystery of the natural world. She has published two nonfiction books.

CORNER THE MARKET

Free Money—or Close to It

Free: what a wonderful word. Most of the time, when I sell a book, it costs me something. I advertise on Facebook, Amazon, and BookBub and pay to promote my books on subscription services such as Written Word Media and The Fussy Librarian. That costs me money, but that's okay because I have a big back catalog and achieve enough organic sales from the new readers my marketing and advertising attracts to make the investments thoroughly worthwhile.

But what if you have only a few books, or the income from your efforts is not yet at a level where you feel that spending money on ads is viable? In this scenario, you need to be doing everything you can without spending money, or you need to be spending small amounts in places that will generate sales.

There are several immediate options, but we're going to focus on two: newsletter swaps and promotional platforms.

NEWSLETTER SWAPS

You need to get your own newsletter set up first, and if you have done that but only have twelve subscribers, you are not offering much value to the people with whom you might swap. Let's assume you have at least a few hundred loyal fans and email them once a month or more. There is nothing stopping you from reaching out to another author in your genre. If their covers are like your covers or their content is like your content, they will be a good target, and your audiences ought to be interested in the work you are swapping.

This costs nothing other than the time it takes you to find the author's email address—probably on their website—and message them.

Target the big names; you have my permission. Chances are JK Rowling won't answer, but you never know if you don't try, and there is no reason not to be persistent, provided you can achieve that without being annoying.

PROMOTIONAL PLATFORMS

There are several promotional platforms you can explore to market your books. BookFunnel and StoryOrigin are the first that come to mind, but there are others out there. With these platforms, you can arrange newsletter swaps with other authors in your genre—meaning you can avoid the approach described above if it makes you feel like a stalker. You have to pay to play, but the fee is only $10 to $20 a month, depending on which tier you choose.

Here, you can also join group promotions. Typically, someone organizes a promotion and invites authors to join. You can narrow your search by genre to find those your titles suit and filter by type of promotion: free, sales, Kindle Unlimited (KU), etc.

Large and In Charge: An All-Genre Giveaway for Stories with Big, Beautiful Women	Kat Samuels	Giveaway	Jul 1, 2022	Aug 1, 2022	Romance Urban Fantasy Women's Fiction Mystery Young Adult
Magical Escapes Fantasy in Kindle Unlimited	C. Gockel	Kindle Unlimited	Jul 1, 2022	Aug 3, 2022	High Fantasy Fairy Tale Paranormal Mythology Urban Fantasy
Free Fantasy & Science Fiction	C. Gockel	Giveaway	Jul 1, 2022	Aug 3, 2022	Space Opera Sci-Fi Urban Fantasy High Fantasy Paranormal
Bloody July: Vampires & Witches 2.99 or less	Theophilus Monroe	Sale	Jul 1, 2022	Aug 3, 2022	Vampires Witches Urban Fantasy Horror Dark
Vanquish the Villains' Romance with Adventure, Mystery Suspense … Twists! PNR, UF, Fantasy, Sci-fi, Fairytale	Sheri-Lynn Marean	Sale	Jul 1, 2022	Aug 1, 2022	Paranormal Fantasy Urban Fantasy Sci-Fi Romance
So Irresistible: Multiple Love Interests, Fantasy Review Copies for Readers!	Everly Reads	Reviews	Jul 2, 2022	Aug 1, 2022	Romance Fantasy Urban Fantasy High Fantasy Epic

Search by genre to find group promotions tailored to your work, then filter your search by the type of promotion to see results like this search in the Urban Fantasy category.

Joining a free group promotion means you will give away a book and have it linked to your newsletter sign-up, so your subscriber numbers will grow. With a sales promo, your book can be at full price or discounted. For each of these and KU promotions, collaborating authors will send links to their newsletters and social media following.

If there are twenty authors with an average of five thousand followers, that's up to one hundred thousand new readers seeing your story in one group promotion.

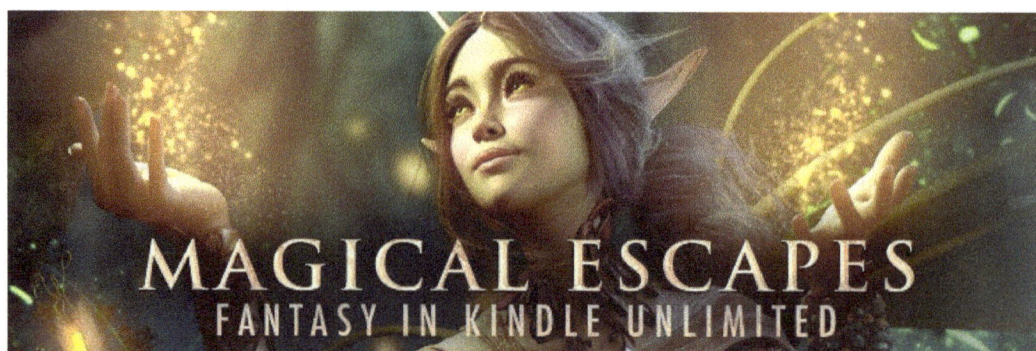

Magical Escapes Fantasy in Kindle Unlimited
Get these books fast! This promotion ends August 3rd!

In group promotions, your title will populate on a landing page alongside the other books in the promotion. This is what you will share on social media and with your newsletter, and what readers will see when they follow the link.

There is no limit to how many group promotions you can join, so imagine the exposure you can get for the price of a cheap lunch, especially when you consider it an investment that will bring you an income. ■

Steve Higgs

Steve Higgs

High school Valedictorian enlists in the Marine Corps under a guaranteed tank contract. An inauspicious start that was quickly superseded by excelling in language study.

STORYTELLER
OPERATING SYSTEM

NOTION FOR AUTHORS

LEARN:

The PARA Method for Writers
Building Your Story Bible
Setting up Books and Series
Task Management for Writing
Task Management for Editing, ARCs, and Betas
Collaborating in Notion
Incorporating Other Apps into Notion
Automating Workflows
And More!

SIGN UP: INDIEAUTHORTRAINING.COM

CLONE YOURSELF

Custom Chat GPT Bots

Harnessing AI's knowledge base and expand your skills and expertise in vital areas such as:

Life and Business Coaching
Mastering Marketing and Newsletter Strategies
Crafting Captivating Blurbs and Social Posts
Enhancing Time Management
Elevating Customer Service
Writing Compelling Ad, Product, and Landing Page Copy

And that's just the beginning.

INDIEAUTHORTRAINING.COM

PUBLISHER ROCKET

FIND
PROFITABLE
KINDLE
KEYWORDS
Book Marketing Research
Made Simple!

writelink.to/pubrocket

www.ingramcontent.com/pod-product-compliance
Lightning Source LLC
Chambersburg PA
CBHW042341030426
42335CB00030B/3429